Affinity Publisher
for
Book Formatting

AFFINITY PUBLISHER FOR

SELF-PUBLISHING

BOOKS 1 AND 4

M.L. HUMPHREY

SELECT TITLES BY M.L. HUMPHREY

AFFINITY PUBLISHER FOR FICTION LAYOUTS

AFFINITY PUBLISHER FOR AD CREATIVES

AFFINITY PUBLISHER FOR BASIC BOOK COVERS

AFFINITY PUBLISHER FOR NON-FICTION

* * *

DATA ANALYSIS FOR SELF-PUBLISHERS

* * *

EXCEL FOR BEGINNERS

WORD FOR BEGINNERS

POWERPOINT FOR BEGINNERS

ACCESS FOR BEGINNERS

CONTENTS

Affinity Publisher for Fiction Layouts   1

Affinity Publisher for Non-Fiction   149

Appendix A: Quick Takes   261

Appendix B: Create A Book From An Existing File   277

Index   279

About the Author   287

Affinity Publisher for Fiction Layouts

AFFINITY PUBLISHER FOR
SELF-PUBLISHING - BOOK 1

M.L. HUMPHREY

CONTENTS

INTRODUCTION   1

A BRIEF INTRODUCTION TO AFFINITY   5

GETTING STARTED WITH PUBLISHER   7

SET UP YOUR WORKSPACE   9

SET UP A NEW FILE TEMPLATE   15

MASTER PAGES   21

SIMPLE TITLE PAGE   25

ADD TITLE PAGE TO THE DOCUMENT   35

CHANGE IMAGE   41

ALSO BY PAGE   43

ADD ALSO BY MASTER PAGE TO DOCUMENT   49

COPYRIGHT AND CHAPTER START MASTER PAGE   53

TEXT AND CHAPTER START MASTER PAGE   61

TEXT AND TEXT MASTER PAGE   65

BUILD THE BEGINNING OF YOUR DOCUMENT   67

TEXT FLOW BETWEEN FRAMES   69

CONTENTS (CONT.)

ADD YOUR MAIN BODY TEXT 75

TEXT STYLES 79

FIRST PARAGRAPH TEXT STYLE 81

MAIN BODY TEXT STYLE 85

CHAPTER HEADING TEXT STYLE 89

APPLY MAIN BODY TEXT STYLE TO ALL 91

ASSESS YOUR APPEARANCE 93

SECTION BREAKS 97

FIND AND REPLACE FOR CHAPTER HEADINGS 99

THE MAIN BODY OF YOUR DOCUMENT 101

APPLY TEXT STYLES 103

APPLY MASTER PAGES 105

MANUALLY FIX WIDOWS AND ORPHANS 109

FIX JUSTIFIED PARAGRAPH ISSUES 113

CREATE MORE MASTER PAGES 115

NO TEXT AND CHAPTER START MASTER PAGE 117

CONTENTS (CONT.)

CHAPTER START AND TEXT MASTER PAGE 119

FIX MISSING ITALICS OR BOLDED TEXT 123

ASSIGN A PAGE ONE 125

TIDY UP 129

ADD BACK MATTER 131

TEXT AND NO TEXT MASTER PAGE 133

NO TEXT AND SECTION START MASTER PAGE 135

FINALIZE BACK MATTER 137

PREFLIGHT 139

EXPORT A PDF 141

REUSE AN OLD BOOK 145

CONCLUSION 147

INTRODUCTION

This book is a guide to walk users through how to create a print layout for a fiction title in Affinity Publisher.

When I first started self-publishing I just used Microsoft Word to format both my ebooks and paperbacks. And there's a certain advantage to using Word that I still think makes it a valid choice for new self-publishers. Most people are already comfortable with it, and as long as you know how to use Styles and Breaks you can put together an acceptable book.

There are obviously a few tricks involved when it comes to using Word for print, and I definitely had a few moments of struggling with page numbering and tables of contents over the years.

For example, if you are doing non-fiction and want a blank even-numbered page before your next chapter start that requires using a section break and then removing the page number in that section only and making sure the page number didn't get edited on any other pages. Annoying, but doable.

So if you're brand new to self-publishing and drowning in everything you need to learn to publish your books, then maybe stick with Word. Or, get Vellum. That's where I went next in my quest to create pretty ebooks and paperbacks. I'm not even a Mac user, but it was worth it to me to spend $250 to get a used Mac to use Vellum on my books and I still use it for my ebooks.

Vellum is a nice, easy-to-use formatting option for both ebook and print. And, trust me, I looked into all those other options that people suggested at the time for ebooks, but Vellum won hands down because it didn't require a ton of expertise to use.

When they came out with their print option I was happy to use that for my novels.

(I never used it for most of my non-fiction because they just didn't have the level of control I want for complex non-fiction that includes sub-sections and images and indexes, etc.)

So, again, if you're new to self-publishing and want to invest in one single software to get started, I'd actually recommend Vellum. It's great for ebook formatting and it'll do the basics for print formatting which is what most self-published authors need when they're getting started.

But if you're like me, you're ultimately going to want more control. I already mentioned my issues with respect to non-fiction and even on the fiction side I personally have an issue with how they handle widows and orphans.

Now, the old-school recommendation is to move to Adobe InDesign at that point. But I did a trial and I didn't like it. I also hate subscription-based software with a passion. Which ultimately led me to Affinity, and Affinity Publisher in particular. One flat fee and a great product.

I've now used it to format probably a hundred or more titles and am still very pleased with it. But there is a learning curve involved.

You can do what I did to learn Affinity Publisher, which is watch the videos they have for free on their website (https://affinity.serif.com/en-us/tutorials/publisher/desktop/), search for help on the internet, and use good old-fashioned trial and error.

That works if you're the type of personality I am who likes to learn that way. I think their videos are excellent. My problem with that approach was that the videos weren't in the order I needed them to be. I didn't have the background to put them into context and some of the videos I most needed to start with—like Master Pages—were much further down on the page so I thought I wasn't going to be able to learn from them.

Another learning option, of course, is this book or the videos I put together on the same topic. The advantage to having this book is that I will walk through from start to finish how I put together a fiction book so everything is in the order (for the most part) that works best for fiction layouts.

I say for the most part because ideally you have all of your Master Pages and Text Styles set up before you begin (and you will after we create your first book), but for me the most intuitive way to build that first book involves a little bit of back and forth setting all of that up. So if that occasional "let's go back and add this bit" moment will throw you then I still may not be the best choice for you.

But if you stick with me, then by the time you finish this book and/or watch the videos, you should have your first fiction book ready to go and have a firm grasp of all of the steps and skills that are needed to create a basic fiction book that includes an accent font, a main body font, and an image that is used in the front matter and chapter headings.

(By the way, a video course that covers the same material as this book is available at ml-humphrey.teachable.com. There's a discount code available at the back of the book for half off the course price. You can also buy a template similar to what we're going to create here through my Payhip store at payhip.com/mlhumphrey, but I do think going through the book and building your first book from scratch is the best way to learn these skills.)

So it's your choice how to learn Affinity Publisher. However you do it, I think it's well worth learning.

Also, if you're new to my books, be advised up front that I am focused in on what you need to know to get this particular job done, so don't expect 100% mastery of every little bell and whistle the program offers. I personally find books like that overwhelming and like to just get right to the meat of what I need to know, but that may not work for all personalities.

Also, the folks at Affinity are continually improving their programs, so what I say now could change. For example, there have been times when I went looking for a functionality in the Affinity suite and it didn't exist but then it was there in the next release. So this is written as of this moment in time (September 2021).

Another note. I am working on a PC so the screenshots you'll see are based on that version of Affinity. Where I use Ctrl shortcuts on an Apple you'd use Command instead.

Finally, I'm going to assume in this book that you can handle the basics of working in a Microsoft Office-style program that has dropdowns and dialogue boxes, etc. (If you don't know what Control shortcuts (like Ctrl + C to copy), dialogue boxes, dropdowns, etc. are then maybe start with my book *Word for Beginners* which defines all of those things. It's obviously for a different software, but that basic functionality and terminology holds across programs and having at least that level of understanding is kind of essential for what we're going to do here.)

I'm also going to assume that you know the basics of formatting for print. If you are brand new to print and don't know anything about anything then maybe check out *Print Books for Beginners* which is available for purchase on my Payhip store in ebook format. (I unpublished it on the wide platforms because the platform information was changing too fast, but the discussion in there about formatting a print book remains unchanged. I'll probably also put up a short video course on that at some point so keep an eye out for that in the Teachable store as well. Check my website mlhumphrey.com for the latest information.)

Alright then. Let's dive in and create a fiction layout for print using Affinity Publisher.

A BRIEF INTRODUCTION TO AFFINITY

The Affinity suite of products can be located at affinity.serif.com. They offer three products, Affinity Photo, Affinity Designer, and Affinity Publisher. Each one has a free trial option so you can see what they're like to work with before you spend your money.

As of the date I'm writing this, each of the three products costs $54.99 in the United States. If you want to wait around they do seem to put them on sale at various points in time throughout the year, but I think that's a very reasonable price for what they offer since it's a one-time payment and you get full updates for that cost.

Again, keeping in mind that I am a self-published author and not a design guru, this is my personal rundown of the three products.

Publisher, which is what we're going to cover in this book, allows you to do multiple-page layouts where text flows across pages. It's also what allows you to insert a table of contents or an index. There are basic design options as well. You can insert images onto pages very easily, for example.

According to their website, Publisher allows you to "combine your images, graphics and text to make beautiful layouts ready for publication."

I also create my covers and advertising images using Publisher. But I will put a little asterisk here because the type of covers I create are basic text and image placement. If you need to do photo manipulation, then you need one of the other Affinity products. Publisher is for putting components into a final layout, not for creating those components.

Designer is the one I use the least and may not even need although I do have it. According to their website it's for creating concept art, print projects, logos, icons, UI designs, mock-ups and more. I can't remember the last time I actually dipped into Designer, but I'd say this is where you combine multiple layers to create really complex images.

Photo is the other Affinity product I do use on occasion. This is the product you need, if, for example, you're going to use layer masks to make your title text on a cover more visible against a background that has a lot of detail. (If you want to learn how to do that and all sorts of other cool things, check out the NeoStock cover design course at https://www.neo-stock.com/core-skills-photoshop-video-training. The course is done in Photoshop but I was able to translate what he discusses there to Affinity.)

You will also use Photo if you ever want to use a mockup file like the ones available for free from CoverVault (https://covervault.com/) that let you create a 3D image of your cover. Even though they're built for Photoshop, Affinity can work with them. Just be sure to change your General Preferences so that "Import PSD smart objects where possible" is checked.

* * *

One of the nice things about Affinity is that if you have all three you can move between Publisher, Designer, and Photo within the same file. They call them personas and they are available in the top left corner of the workspace. So any time you're in Publisher, for example, and you need to do something that's only possible in Designer or Photo, you can just click on the "persona" for the other program and the workspace will change and give you the options for that program without you having to close the file or import or export.

Now that you have that background, we're going to focus in on Publisher, because that's all you should need for putting together a beautiful fiction layout for print.

GETTING STARTED WITH PUBLISHER

Okay then. I'm going to assume here that you've gone to the Affinity website and downloaded Affinity Publisher and have opened it.

If you have a lot of fonts, like I do thanks to my font addiction which has been fed by cheaply-priced Design Cuts bundles (https://www.designcuts.com/), then Affinity may be slow to load.

My computer is pretty fast, but on the one where I have all of my fonts accessible, it takes about ten times longer to load Affinity as it does on my computer where I moved the fonts I really don't use into a different folder.

So if Affinity is slow to start and you have lots of fonts and that bugs you, move the fonts you don't use to a different folder.

Once Affinity loads, you should see something similar to this:

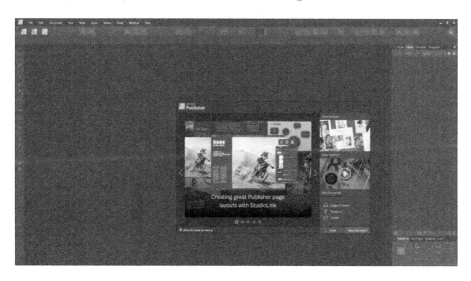

Personally I like to set my workspace up a little differently, so let's cover that next. Click on Close to get rid of that Affinity Publisher welcome screen and then let's go set up your studio presets.

SET UP YOUR WORKSPACE

I prefer to arrange my workspace differently depending on whether I'm doing a cover design or working on the interior of a book. Especially since I do a lot of non-fiction interiors that involve images and indexes, etc. So before we begin I want to walk you through how to make your workspace look like the one I'm going to be using from here on out.

To do that, you have to understand that Affinity works with what they call studios. The full range of studios can be found by going to View at the top of the screen, clicking on that, and then taking your mouse down to Studio. This brings up a secondary dropdown menu with a number of listed options.

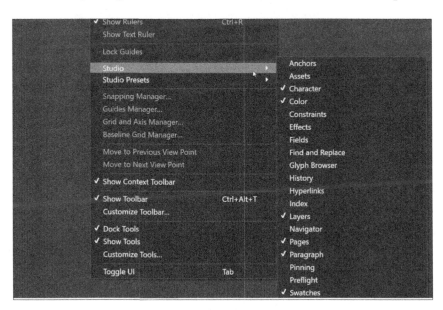

You can see that some, like Character and Color, are checked. And some, like Preflight, are not. The ones that are checked are already visible in your workspace. The ones that are not checked are not visible by default. Character is on the top right in the default view and Color is on the bottom right in the default view, for example, but to use Preflight you'd have to specifically open it.

A studio is basically a task pane that you can click on to see various options related to that topic. We're not going to dig too deep into that right this second, because you're going to learn all about those options later by seeing and doing. For now, just accept that each studio gives you different options and that for creating a print interior I want you to have certain studios available in your workspace.

Now it's time to arrange our workspace with the studios we're going to use and to put them where I find they work the best for me.

The first thing I want you to do is go to your main workspace and on the top right-hand side find the tab for Pages. Left-click on it and drag it over to the left-hand side of your workspace. If you drag it to a point where it overlaps with the left-hand set of menu choices it should flash blue and have an outline.

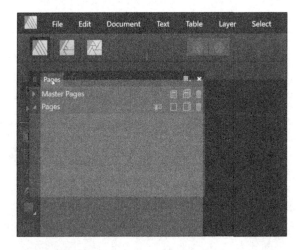

Let go at that point and the studio should move to that side of your workspace and "dock" so that it's fixed to that point now.

Next I want you to add the Find and Replace, Table of Contents, Index, Preflight, Fields, and Text Styles studios. For each one, go to View, go down to Studio, and then select it. This will either add that studio as a tab next to your existing studios or it will open as a standalone dialogue box on top of the workspace.

If they open as standalone dialogue boxes, you'll end up with something that looks like this with all of the studios open on top of your workspace:

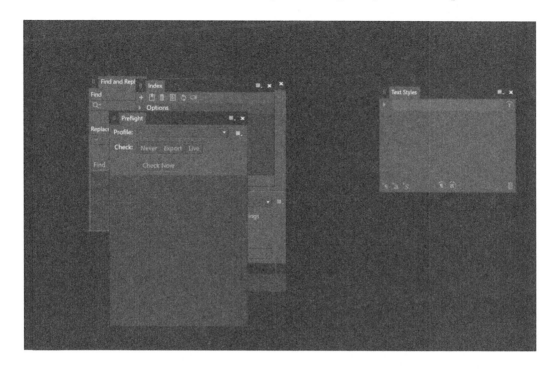

We need to place those studios somewhere we can access them easily but where they aren't in the way.

Left-click on Text Styles and drag it over to where the Layers, Character, and Paragraph studios are on the top right-hand side of your screen. When you do so it should get added to that set of tabs. Drag it to the end and let go. It should now look like this:

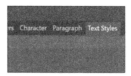

See how Text Styles is listed at the end of that row of options? Now add Fields to the same section.

Next, click and drag Find and Replace next to Pages so that you have two tabs in that section. Then do the same for Table of Contents, Index, and Preflight.

When you're done, you'll have a workspace that looks like this where I currently have the Pages studio selected on the left-hand side and the Layers studio selected on the right-hand side.

You can click on each tab to see the options available for that particular studio, but can only see the options for one studio in each section at a time. That's why I like to have my Pages studio on the left-hand side so that it's almost always visible while I'm working in my text studios on the right-hand side.

This is how I personally like to have my workspace set up when working with print layouts, but you can set it up any way you want. If you're doing only fiction, for example, you may not need to have an index so you may want to close that out.

Or if you don't plan to have a table of contents (which our example isn't going to have) you may want to close that. But these are the studios I find myself using the most when doing print layouts and they're the ones you'll see in the screenshots in the rest of this book.

When you exit Affinity and come back in, it will give you the last workspace layout you were using. So if you only have one way in which you want to use Affinity, you can simply set it up and exit and Affinity will retain that layout.

For cover design, however, I use a very different layout from my print design layout. Rather than recreate this layout each and every time, I use studio presets that let me move back and forth between my two workspaces.

To save a layout as a studio preset, click on the View option in the top menu, go to Studio Presets, and choose Add Preset.

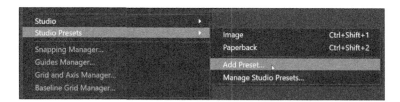

This will bring up a dialogue box which asks you to provide a name for your preset studio layout. I call mine Paperback. So type that into the box and then choose OK.

If you then go back to the View, Studio Presets option, you can see all of your available presets. So in the image above you can see that I have Paperback and Image to choose from.

To change over to your preferred preset, simply click on the one you want. Or you can see in the image above that Affinity automatically assigns each preset a Control shortcut of Ctrl + Shift + [a number].

For the curious, this is how I have the top right corner for my Image workspace arranged:

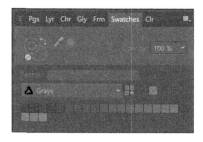

I've moved the Color, Swatches, and Text Frame studios up and also added the Glyph Browser. I have Transform by itself down below and have nothing on the left-hand side.

The main focus for me when working on images is the Layers studio. For book formatting it's the Pages studio.

One more thing before we move on from studio presets and that's how to change one. As far as I can tell there is not a save feature for when you update existing presets, but what does work is to save a new preset using the old name.

When you do that and click OK it then asks if you want to replace the existing studio preset that has that name and you can say Yes. Done.

Alright. Now that we've set up our workspace, it's time to move on to setting up our file.

SET UP A NEW FILE TEMPLATE

The next step is to set up your new file for a print paperback. Depending on the type of book you're writing this will vary. So, for example, when I publish a novel I use a 5.25 by 8 inch size with certain margin settings. But when I publish that same novel in large print I use a 6 by 9 inch size with different margins. And when I publish non-fiction computer books I use 7.5 by 9.25 inch.

When in doubt about your settings, I always recommend starting with the print book templates provided by Amazon. They download as a Word file, but then you can open that file and go to Page Layout-> Margins-> Custom Margins to see how they've set up their margins for that specific size.

Keep in mind that print books use something called mirrored margins, meaning that the outer left and outer right margins are the same and the inner left and inner right margins are the same. The inner margin tends to be larger and to also include what's called a gutter which allows room for binding the pages together without cutting off the text.

If you're going to do this more than once you can create a preset for each size. (Although what I tend to do is open the last book of that size that I did and just delete out the text from the last book and replace it with my new text. I do this because then the master pages, etc. are all the way I want them already. But for ad templates I do have presets, simply because I'm too lazy to remember all the various sizes that are required for all the different ad types.)

Anyway. Go to File-> New or if you just opened Affinity click on New Document from the welcome screen. This will bring up the New Document dialogue box. There are default print sizes listed, but I don't use them because they're not what I need.

For example, here I've clicked on Print and then Letter and you can see on the right-hand side that this is for an 8.5 x 11 inch document with a DPI of 300, that the unit size is in inches, that it is a portrait orientation and images are going to be embedded and it's also one page. The color format is also RGB/8. Scroll down more and you'll see information about the margins and any bleed.

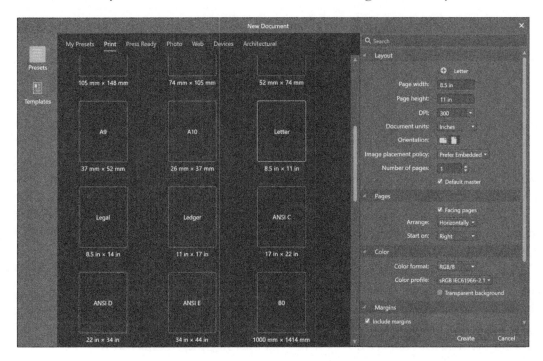

What I recommend is finding this existing template or another that's in inches and then editing it. We're going to do that to create something that will work for a 5.25 x 8 inch book.

First, click onto the 8.5 x 11 inch template. Next, click into page width and change that to 5.25 and then tab to the next field. (As soon as you do that the Layout name just above that field will change to Custom, because it's no longer that existing template.)

Next, change the page height to 8 and make sure the DPI is 300 or more. For fiction this isn't as important, but if you want to put your cover image at the front of the book or if you want an image for each chapter start or for your section dividers then you ideally want this set to 300 DPI or more. If it isn't the image may be blurry. (Not horribly so, but it's easy enough to address here so why not do it?)

Plus it saves you getting an alert from IngramSpark when you upload your file. (Assuming that the images you place remain 300 DPI after you've placed them. Affinity can't fix the nature of a small image.)

OK. 5.25, 8, 300 (or a little more if you want), inches, portrait. (If you ever do a picture book or something like that you may need to change this to landscape, but even then it may be fine.)

Image placement can go either way. For fiction it only matters if you plan to include an image, which our template does, so this setting does matter to us. I'm going to use Linked.

Linking the image saves file size and if you use a handful of different images in a file Affinity is going to ask if you'd rather link than embed anyway. Also, if you're linked instead of embedded, Affinity will warn you when you update the image outside of the program and ask if you want to update the image within your file which can be a useful reminder that you need to do so. And it makes it easier to swap out an image if you use it multiple times in your document and choose to use a different one later.

One drawback to linked is that if you move the image from where it's saved and don't update you'll have a blurred space where that image should be instead of the image itself in your document.

Next, I always set it to have a number of pages of 1. I then add more pages using Master Pages, which we'll discuss soon.

And you want facing pages, arranged horizontally, that start on the right.

I recommend using Gray/8 as your color. This will transform any color image you put into the document into a grayscale image which is what you're going to want for most titles. (As a print-on-demand self-publisher the cost of a color book is generally too high to bother with.) Gray/16 can work as well, but interestingly enough last time I checked Ingram wanted 8 not 16. This is another one that's really only relevant if you use images.

Margins. For a 5.25 by 8 book I have mine set to .9 inch for the inner margin, .6 inch for the outer margin, and .76 inches for the top and bottom margins.

I also have bleed set on my books of .125 inches for each side. To be honest, I'm not sure I need it and I'm pretty sure the export option I choose drops it out. But I just keep it there in case.

(The only time bleed really comes up is if you're using Affinity Publisher with one of the KDP cover templates, because they do have bleed and you do need to remember to export your file with bleed included or else Amazon will tell you that the cover isn't the right size.)

Back to this new document. If you're not going to use it again, click Create and it will create a new document for you using those parameters.

If you do want to use it again, then you need to create a preset template. To do that, go back to the top of your options and click on the + sign next to Custom. This will add the preset you just created to the My Presets section with a name of Unnamed 1 (or whatever number you're up to if you haven't named your presets).

Right-click on that thumbnail and choose Rename Preset and type in the name you want. Be sure to choose a name that is descriptive enough that you'll know what the file is. I prefer to include size information and purpose.

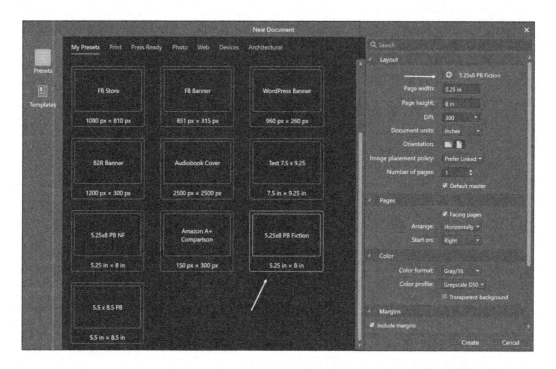

In the image above you can see my new 5.25x8 PB Fiction preset in the bottom right corner and that that name is also showing on the top right-hand side above all of my parameters.

As a side note, you can see the other templates I have in there. I have presets for Facebook ads, ebook covers, BookBub ads, Facebook banners, etc. Creating these in advance makes it much easier to just open Affinity and create a new ad without having to go dig for the required dimensions.

Before we move on from here, let me just touch on large print for a minute.

For my large print books I use a 6 by 9 size. So inches are 6 and 9. And I increase the size of my margins to a 1 inch inner margin, a .75 inch outer margin, and a .9 inch top and bottom margin. Otherwise, the settings remain unchanged.

Okay.

Once you're done with your settings, click on Create. You will get something that looks like this.

It should look like a page of the book you want to create. That blue border in the center is the area where we've told Affinity text will go. The white space around it is the space for your margins. That blue border in the black space around the perimeter is the area for the bleed which, as I mentioned before, I'm not sure you actually need but it doesn't hurt to include.

It can be tempting at this point to try to type into that space. The next step is to add text, right? But no. We still need to lay groundwork with our Master Pages and Text Styles.

MASTER PAGES

For me, master pages are the core of what makes using Affinity Publisher so much better than using Word for print formatting.

Master pages are basically templates that you create that include your page numbering, your headers, your footers, any images you want on the page, and your text placement.

I create a master page for every type of two-page spread I need in a book.

Applying master pages is probably 75% of the formatting work of creating a book. Combine that with text styles, which we'll talk about shortly, and you're probably 90% of the way there.

Ideally.

For the fiction book we're going to create here, I have nine master pages. There's the title page, the also by page, the copyright and chapter start page, and the about the author page. And then there are the master pages for the main body text which include all of the combinations of chapter start and text (text and chapter start, chapter start and text, no text and chapter start, text and text, and text and no text).

For any given book you may not use all of those, but it's nice to have them if you need them and they're pretty easy to put together. (I think you can actually do your master pages in one-page spreads instead which would mean having a text, a chapter start, and a no text master page, but then you'd also have to apply them one at a time and I don't think it saves all that much effort so we're going to be building two-page master pages here.)

It probably sounds a little complicated right now, so let's just dive in and start building. I'm going to assume from here on out that you built your workspace to look like mine and I'll give directions based on that fact. If you didn't, then you'll need to adjust accordingly.

So.

Go to the top left corner of your workspace where we pinned the Pages studio and click on it. You should see two sections, one for Master Pages and one for Pages. Click on Master Pages to expand that section. It should look like this once you do:

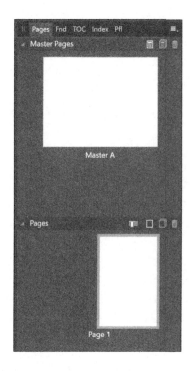

Double-click on that Master A thumbnail in the Master Pages section and you will see that master in the main workspace where you can now edit it.

But first, go back to the Master A thumbnail and click on its name. This should highlight the name in blue. Type in the name you want for this master page and click enter. I'm going to name this first master page "Simple Title Page."

If your view has small thumbnails in it where the name is off to the side instead of below the thumbnail, I'd recommend you change that. To do so, be sure that you have the Pages studio selected and then go to the top right corner of that section (right above the trash can) and click on the image with four lines and a little dropdown arrow on the right-hand side.

This will bring up a dropdown menu where you can change the option from Small to Large.

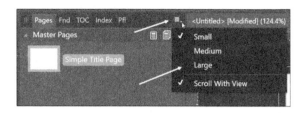

Much better. Much easier to see the difference between your master pages with just a glance.

Of course, right now, there's only one master page and it's blank so there's not much to see. Let's change that.

SIMPLE TITLE PAGE

Go to the main workspace where you should see a larger version of your master page. (If not, double-click on the thumbnail to bring it up.)

Right now, this page has no elements on it. You can see two blue borders that designate our "text area", but the page itself is not yet set up with text frames to hold text. It's more like a sketch of our basic format so we know where to place our elements, but none of what you see right now will appear on your final document. And if we added text directly onto this page right now it would not in any way be constrained to those text areas.

That's what we're doing when we build master pages. We're adding the elements that we want to use on each page. For this simple title page, that's going to be a text frame and an image. What we ultimately want on this page should look like this:

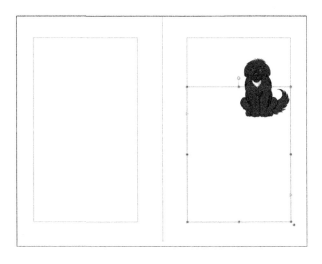

Obviously you can add whatever design elements you want. For this guide, I'm going to walk you through a fairly simple layout that I've used in the past for my cozy mystery series that includes a few little embellishments that highlight what you can do with Affinity but that also doesn't take much effort.

So from here on out I'll be recreating the layout for *A Dead Man and Doggie Delights*, the first book in that series, so you can see what we're doing applied to real content. The image I use in those books is that Newfoundland dog that you see in the screenshot above.

To create the title page, the first thing we want to do is add the text frame. To do this, click on the capital T on the left-hand-side panel of options to select the Frame Text Tool. This will let you create a box on the page where you can then place text.

After you select the tool, when you hold your cursor over the workspace you'll see that you now have a little T in a box hanging out next to your cursor. Go to the right-hand page of your workspace and left-click and drag to form a text frame that aligns with the blue outline on the right, left, and bottom edges.

I click on the left-hand edge of the frame and then drag down and over.

As you drag the text frame into place, you will see green or red lines when the frame aligns with your existing boundaries. So in the picture below you can see that there is a red line where I've dragged the frame down to the bottom boundary and a green one along the right side. This means I've created a text frame that fills the space I wanted to use for placing text in my document.

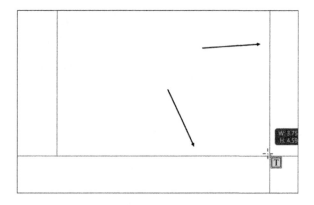

If you don't see any red or green lines as you drag your text frame into alignment, then you need to turn on Snapping. This can be done by going to the top menu and clicking on the dropdown arrow next to the image that looks like a red horseshoe magnet. In the menu that appears when you do that make sure that the Enable Snapping box at the top is checked.

For the main text on a page, you want any text frames that you place in your master pages to line up with the template boundaries we established for our text. (Remember, this is for creating a basic fiction book layout. If this were a magazine spread, that might not be the case.)

If you don't get it right immediately, that's okay. You can always click on the text frame again to select it, and then click and drag from the blue circles along the perimeter to resize the frame.

Below I've created a text frame that goes too far to the right and the bottom to show how this works.

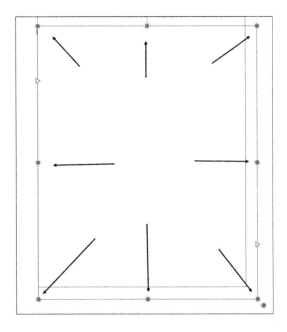

I clicked on the frame, and you can see its outline using the blue circles in the corners and along each edge. It's a little confusing because the line for the text area in the template is also blue, but those circles along the edge and at the corners are the best indicators of which lines belong to the text frame.

The text frame I inserted is aligned with the text area on the left-hand side, but not on the other three sides.

To align the text frame with the bottom and right-hand edges, I can left-click on the circle in the bottom right corner and drag left and up until I see the red and green lines that tell me I'm aligned with the template frame like in the screenshot I initially showed you above.

When you get the text frame aligned with the text area in the template, the blue circles will also turn red or green.

Once you do this, let up on the left-click, and your text frame will be aligned with the underlying template frame.

Now we have something else to fix.

The text frame I just drew isn't the height I want for this page. I don't want it all the way to the top, but I do want it to be taller than this. And because I want to make sure that I use the same height across my master pages for visual continuity, I'm going to adjust this via the Transform studio.

The Transform studio is in the bottom right corner. Click on that tab. The current width of my text frame (W) is 3.75 and the current height (H) is 4.594.

What we want to fix is the H value.

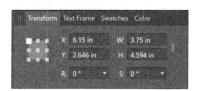

I want a height of 4.75, so I click into the H box and I change the value to what I want and then hit enter.

The increase in height was added to the bottom of the frame, which means it's no longer aligned with my template. I can easily fix this by clicking and dragging the text frame up so that it's within the boundaries of the template once more.

How to do this will depend on whether you have the Move Tool selected or a different tool selected.

You likely have the Text Frame Tool still selected, which means you can hold your mouse over the top edge of the text box until it turns into a four-sided arrow and then click and drag the text frame into alignment.

If you instead had the Move Tool selected then the four-sided arrow won't appear, but you can left-click anywhere on the text frame and drag into place.

(Reminder: click and drag means you left-click and hold that left-click as you move your cursor which should also move the selected object. Also, from here on out, if I just say to click, assume that means left-click.)

If you don't want to also include an image on your title page, that would be it. You now have a master page where you can type in your title on the right-hand page and there will be no headers, footers, page numbers, etc. that appear on that page or the opposite page.

But let's go ahead now and add an image. As I showed you above, I have a simple black and white image of the Newfoundland dog I use on my covers that I want to add to the right-hand corner of that text frame.

To add your image, click on the icon with a picture of mountains on it from the left-hand set of options. (It will show as the Place Image Tool if you hover your mouse over it.)

This will bring up an Open dialogue box where you can then navigate to and select the image you want to use. Once you've done so, click Open.

For me when I did that it automatically put the image in the text frame because I hadn't clicked away from it.

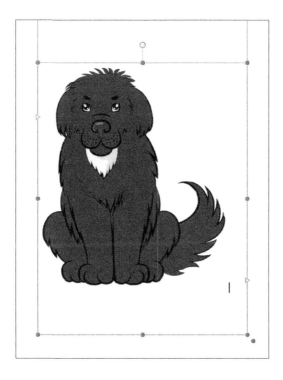

But I don't actually want that. I want my image to be separate from my text frame.

If this happens to you, go to the Layers studio on the top right-hand side of the screen and click on the arrow on the left-hand side for that text frame layer to expand it.

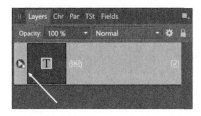

When you expand the text frame layer, you'll see a separate layer for the image that's shown as a subset of the text frame layer.

(I've made the thumbnails here large so they're easier to see. It's the same method as we used for the Pages studio thumbnails.)

Because I don't want that image as a sub item in the text layer, I need to unpin the image.

If you look very closely at the image layer, you'll see that on the right-hand side there is a checkbox. And to the left of that is a white box with lines around it. (It's kind of hard to see, but it's there. I have an arrow pointing to it in the screenshot above.) Click on that white box with lines.

This will open the Pinning studio. From there click on Unpin.

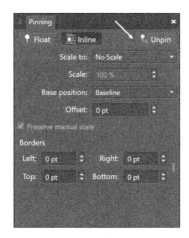

When you unpin the image, this will separate the image layer from the text frame layer. They will both still show in the Layers studio, but will now show as independent of one another.

(You could have also just clicked on the image layer, opened the Pinning studio using the View-> Studio option in the top menu and unpinned that way as well.)

* * *

Of course, it is possible to not have to go through that whole unpinning mess. That happened to me because I was still clicked onto that text frame layer when I tried to insert the image. But I wanted to walk through how to fix it in case it happened to you, too, since it was the default outcome based on the steps we'd already followed.

(I can't tell what will go wrong for you in your book creation process, but I can pretty much guarantee that something will go wrong. Don't panic when that happens. Affinity has good help and internet searches for Affinity instructions also work well. And you can always reach out to me if you get stuck, too.)

* * *

Okay. To avoid that process of having to unpin your image from the Text Frame, before you insert the image click on the Move Tool black arrow at the top of the left-hand set of icons. Then click on the image tool. That will ensure that you're not still in the text frame tool when you insert the image.

If you then click on the Place Image Tool, rather than Affinity inserting the image for you, you'll see a weird little shape next to your cursor that looks like an arrow pointing down at a blue and white circle.

Left-click and drag on the right-hand side of your workspace where you want to place the image. As you click and drag, you should see your image appear on the page. Drag until it's approximately the size you want.

The screenshot above shows the image as well as the cursor in the bottom-right corner.

The image should insert proportionately, meaning it won't stretch or skew as you put the image into your document, and it should appear as its own standalone layer in the Layers studio.

Once the image is inserted into the document you can move it around by left-clicking on it and dragging or left-clicking on the layer in the Layers studio and then left-clicking and dragging.

Once the image has been clicked on you can also use the arrow keys to move it around rather than dragging with the mouse.

To change the dimensions you can drag from the corner or use the Transform section.

If you want to keep the height and width proportionate, the best bet is to use the Transform section and click on the Lock Aspect Ratio option to the right side of the W and H boxes. It looks like two little links connected by a center bar. When it's locked it will have lines going between the W and H boxes and any change to W will also change H or vice versa.

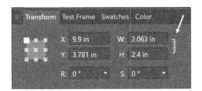

You can use the blue circles around the perimeter of the image to change the size, however doing so will stretch the image out of shape. (Remember, just like in Microsoft Office, Ctrl + Z, Undo, is your friend.)

If you think you accidentally stretched an image, but it's not blatantly obvious you can check that in the Preflight studio that we placed on the top left-hand side. According to Affinity you can use Shift and double-click one of the side handles to return the image to a proportionate size, but I just adjust the image until that warning in the Preflight studio goes away.

I want to position this image so that it is aligned on the right-hand side of the text area and centered along the top edge of my text frame. Like so:

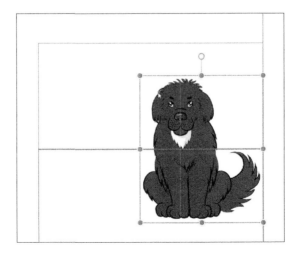

See the red line through the center and the green line along the right-hand edge? That's what I want.

Okay. So that's it. That's the first master page. We have our text frame and our image. But no actual text. And here's why:

In any master page, you don't want to include text or images on that master page that you wouldn't want to see on every single page in your document that uses that master page.

So since the only text I want on this page is the book title and that will vary each time I create a book for this series, I don't want to put the book title on my master page. On the next master page we create, the Also By page, I am going to have the text because it's the same across all of the books. But for this page, no.

(It's not the end of the world if you do put the title on the page now, you'll just have to replace it in the Pages section each time, which could impact carrythrough of any updates you make to that master page.)

ADD TITLE PAGE TO THE DOCUMENT

Once you have your title page ready, it's time to add it to your actual document. You do this in the Pages section of the Pages studio.

Let's look at that now. This is the Pages studio with both our Master Pages and Pages versions of this first page.

Right now, they look the same.

In the Master Pages section we have the Simple Title Page we just created. You can't see the text box, but it's there. You can see the image we inserted. Same for the first page in the Pages section which by default uses this master page because it's the only one

In the Pages section you only see the right-hand side, because when we set up our document we told Affinity to start the document on the right-hand side.

Now it's time to add our book title which we want to do in the document we're creating, so in the Pages section. Double-click on that single-page thumbnail.

The page that you now see in the workspace should be that first single page from the Pages section.

We want to add text to it. To do so, click on the A from the left-hand menu which is the Artistic Text Tool. Next, click into the text frame on the page and type in your title. Like so:

But that doesn't work at all, does it? The text is way too small for the space. Plus I want to use a different font.

Use Ctrl + A to select all of the text you just typed. Now go to the top left menu and you'll see dropdowns where you can change the font, font weight, and font size.

(If you don't see the font dropdown options make sure you have the text layer selected as well as the text tool selected.)

Okay. For this series I use a font called Brushability Sans and on this page I like to use the Light weight in a 30 point size. Font selection works just like it would in Word. You can start typing the font name into the dropdown menu field or scroll down to the one you want.

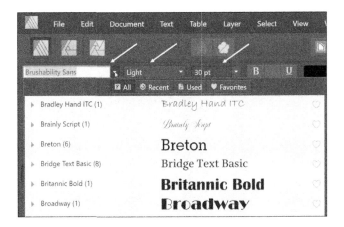

(You probably won't have Brushability Sans as a font choice but if you want practice changing out your fonts, you can use Calibri instead.)

After I make that change, I now have this:

It still has an issue though, right? Because the text is still going across the image and you can't read it.

At this point it might be tempting to just use Enter to create line breaks to get that text to no longer touch the image we inserted. But you don't have to do that.

And you don't *want* to either, because if you do that you're fixing the problem once with a manual solution. Better to fix it forever with an automated solution.

So to fix this, go back to the Master Page section. Double-click on the thumbnail for the title page, click on the Move Tool, and then click on the image or just click on the layer for the image in the Layers studio.

Now go to the top set of menu options and click on the Show Text Wrap Settings icon (indicated by the arrow at the top of the screenshot below). This will bring up the Text Wrap dialogue box.

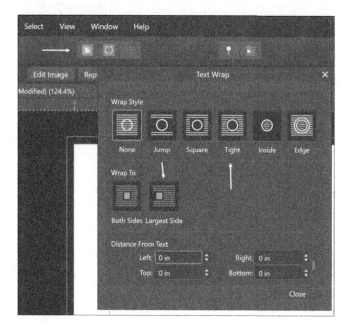

In this particular case, the options we want to click on are a Wrap Style of Tight and then Wrap To Largest Side. (See arrows above.)

What that's going to do is wrap the text around the image on the left-hand side because that's the side that has the most space, and it's going to keep the text close to the image and still on the same line but without overlapping it.

As you can see in that dialogue box, there are other options available. We'll use one of them on the next master page.

And here's what we get automatically in our document as a result of that change:

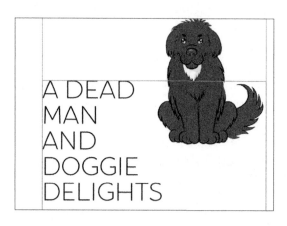

Now, why did we do this in the master? One, because Affinity won't let us do it on an actual page since the image was originally placed onto the master, so we had no real choice. But, two, because that means this formatting we just applied will always apply to the use of this master page. You won't have to think about it again. Every title you type into that title page in the Pages section, the text will automatically flow around the image.

(You may need to think about the optics of how it flows. With my cozy mystery series I found that a title later in the series that had longer words in it flowed differently and I had to adjust my font size to make it look good, but the actual flowing of the text around the image will not be an issue again.)

So that was our first master page completed.

A quick note before we move on.

While you're working on your document, if you ever want to see what a page is going to look like when it's printed without having to generate a PDF, look at that page in the Pages section. The workspace will show lines that aren't going to appear in the final, but the thumbnails should always look like your final product.

Okay. That probably seemed like a lot, but the good news is you only have to create this once for each series and if you stick to a similar layout for your other series it's not a lot of work to update. Let me show you just how easy it can be.

CHANGE IMAGE

Let's say that for another series I don't want a Newfoundland dog on the title page, but instead I want a bulldog in a top hat. By the time we're done here we'll have seven different master pages that use that image. But the nice thing is you don't have to change each of those seven pages individually. You can use the resource manager and change them all at once.

To do that, go to Document at the top of the screen and choose Resource Manager from the dropdown menu. This will bring up the Resource Manager dialogue box.

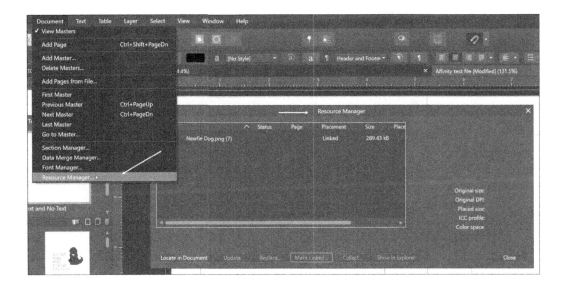

If your images are linked and you've used multiple versions of an image, you will see the image listed with an arrow next to it. You can click on that arrow to see each usage of the image. But you can also, for our purposes, just click on that row for the image you want to replace and then click on the Replace option down below.

Navigate to where the new image you want to use is located, click on it, and click on Open.

Your document should now have the new image in place of the old one in each location it was used as you can see here:

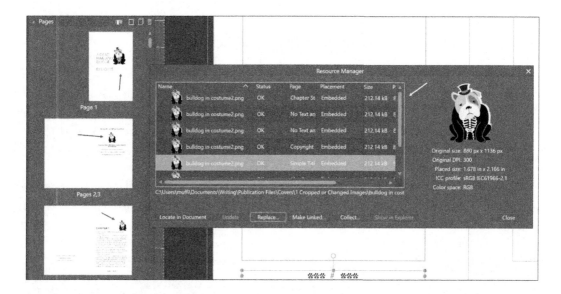

This approach should work as long as you haven't done any fancy work on the image in the Affinity file itself. I recently ran into a situation where it didn't work but I think that was because I'd applied Layer Masks to the image using Affinity Photo.

For what we're doing here though, you should be fine.

So if you set up a template that can work across multiple series with an image as part of the template, then it's only a matter of a minute or two to swap out the image for Series 1 and replace it with the image for Series 2. (Especially if you use images that are the same dimensions so you don't have to click and drag to adjust the images on each of the master pages.)

Now on to the rest of the master pages we want to create. Next up is the Also By page.

ALSO BY PAGE

The next master page we want to create is the Also By page. It looks like this:

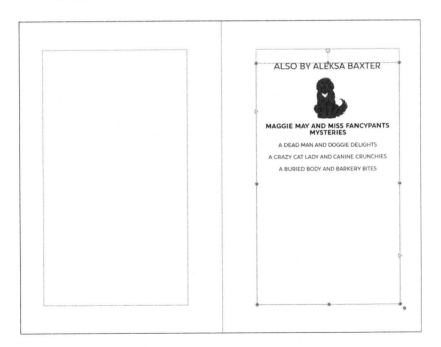

There are three components, a text frame, an image, and text.

You could technically just set up a master page with a blank text box and image and then add your also by text in the Pages section instead, but I prefer to add it here since it's the same across all of the books in the series.

(And if you download one of the templates I've created for others to use you'll see that I've put filler text in this section that can still be edited from the Pages section so I see no reason not to put text on this particular page.)

Okay. First thing we need to do is to create a new master page.

To do that, go to the Master Pages section of the Pages studio and right-click on your existing master page. In the dropdown menu choose Duplicate.

(Insert Master would also work, but it makes for an additional step since we're not changing any of the dimensions or margins compared to our existing master page.)

Duplicate creates an exact copy of the master page you right-clicked on, name and all.

The first thing we want to do is rename the new master page. So scroll down to that newly-created duplicate, click on it, and then click on the name.

The name should now be highlighted in blue.

Type in the name you want (I use Also By) and hit Enter.

Now double-click on the thumbnail image of the master page you just renamed because you want to be sure you're making edits to the right version of the master page. (I can't count the number of times I duplicated a master page, renamed it, and made edits only to realize I'd ended up making those edits to the original and not the copy because I failed to double-click on the correct master page thumbnail.)

Once you've done this, you should have two master pages that are identical in terms of content, but have different names.

Because we copied the title page, we already have a text frame and image in our also by master page. So all we need to do is change the size of the frame, change the size of the image, center and move the image, change the text wrap style, and then add our text.

To change the size of the text frame, go to the Layers studio on the right-hand side and click on the Frame Text layer. This is going to outline that text frame and show the blue circles around the perimeter.

Click and drag the top line of the text frame upward to where you want your also by text to start. My text frame ended up being about six inches tall when I was done because I didn't want the text to start at the top of my text area but I did want it higher than my title page text.

Another option for changing the height of the text frame is to click on it and then use the Transform studio instead. But then you'll have to drag the frame back into place because Affinity adds the height to the bottom not the top.

That's the text frame resized. Next the image.

Click on that layer and this time you can click and drag from the corner at an angle to resize the image while keeping it proportionate.

Your other option is to use the Transform studio. Click on the image, make sure to lock the aspect ratio, and then enter your new value for height or width.

For this page I made the image smaller. It was 2.166 inches high on the title page and here I made it 1.4 inches high.

Once the image is the size you want it, it's time to move and center it. Click on the image and drag it to where you want it to be.

As you drag the image around, you should see green or red lines appear (assuming you've turned on snapping, which you should) as it is centered within one of the pages or frames or aligned with the edge of one of the pages or frames.

What you want is for the image to be centered in your text frame, like it is below, and with enough space above it for there to be a line of 16 point text:

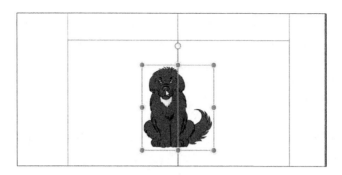

When you center the image, be careful that you are actually aligned to the space you want to be aligned to. Affinity will show when you're centered both on the page and within the text frame. Because print books use a larger interior margin than exterior margin those will not be the same.

So when you move your image around you will see a green line appear indicating the image is centered two separate times. You want the green line that appears when the image is centered in the text frame. You should be able to visually identify this by making sure that the white space on both sides of the image is the same width within that frame as you can see in the screenshot above.

Note that there are alignment options available in the top menu in Affinity, but I prefer to click and drag and use the snapping lines instead for print layouts because of this issue.

(I also might actually move this image off-center if I were trying to create a final book using it, because Affinity is using the frame around the image to center it and as you can see with this image the center of the body of the dog is to the left of the center of the overall image so even though it is technically centered it might not feel that way to a reader.)

Anyway. Place your image where you want it and then it's time to add the text.

Click on the A on the left-hand side and then click into the top of the text box and type the first line of text, in this case "Also By [Author Name]" where [Author Name] is whatever your author name is. Hit Enter.

Format that line with your chosen font and font size. I'm going to use Brushability Sans, Regular, 16 pt. And I want to center this text, which is an option available in the top menu in the center section. Align Center is the second choice.

(It's also available at the top of the Paragraph studio.)

Even though the text will probably look like it's too close to the top of the text frame, it's okay because that text frame line will not exist in the final product. You can see that if you look at the thumbnail of this page on the left under the Master Pages section.

In order to make sure that the next line of text appears below our image instead of across it, we now need to go back to the image and change the text wrap settings.

So click on the image layer (or click on the Move Tool and then the image in the workspace). Next, click on the Show Text Wrap Settings option up top, and then in the Text Wrap dialogue box choose Jump.

Go back to your text tool and click on your text and make sure that the cursor for your second line of text is below the image but that the also by text remains above the image. Like so:

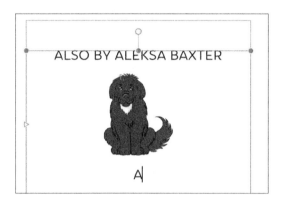

If not, use the Move Tool to move the image until that is the case.

(Because we used Jump for the text wrap setting on that image, the text you add will always be either above or below the image but never on the same line as the image. So you're looking for that sweet spot where the first line of text doesn't have to jump the image, but the second line does.)

Now it's time to add the series title and books for this author. I'm going to type that all in first and then format it.

I want *Maggie May and Miss Fancypants Mysteries* for the series name and then I'm going to list the first three titles in the series, *A Dead Man and Doggie Delights, A Crazy Cat Lady and Canine Crunchies,* and *A Buried Body and Barkery Bite*s.

The font will stay the same and the text will stay centered, but I want the series name bolded (Ctrl + B or click on the B in the top menu) and 12 pt. And then the titles regular 10 pt.

For now I'm just going to manually format these lines. Ultimately it's a best practice to have text styles assigned to each of these different lines and I do that in the template, but I don't want to bog us down right this second with learning text styles. So we're going to table that for the time being and just manually format our text.

And that's it. We now have an Also By master page that looks like this:

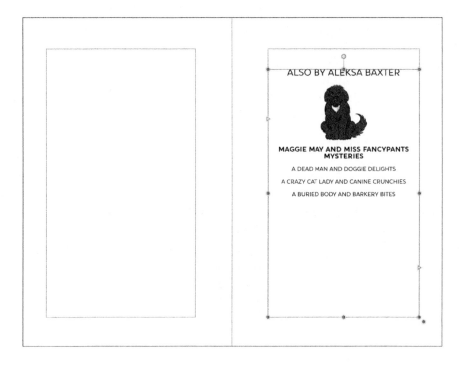

I'd probably tweak that a little more if I was publishing this, but it gives you an idea at least.

ADD ALSO BY MASTER PAGE TO DOCUMENT

We now have two master pages, but in the actual Pages section we still have just the one title page. To add in our also by section, we need to add two pages to our document and then apply the Also By master page to them.

To do that, go to the Pages section, and right-click on the thumbnail for the title page. From the dropdown that appears choose Add Pages.

This will bring up the Add Pages dialogue box. Choose to add 2 pages, After, Page 1, and from the Master Page dropdown menu select the Also By master page.

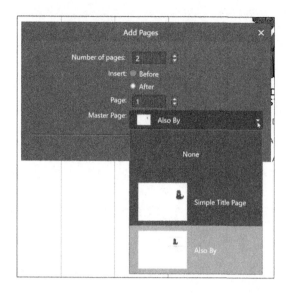

Click OK, and here we go:

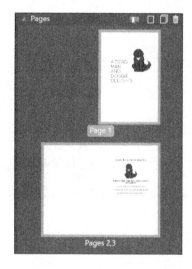

Our document, which is what's shown in the Pages section, now has a title page as well as the two-page Also By spread.

You can edit the text on the Also By page in the Pages section or in the Master Pages section. But if there's ever a typo or another permanent fix you need to make, it's best to fix it in the Master Pages section. This is because of how changes made in one section impact the other.

Changes made in the Pages section will not carry back to the Master Pages section.

But changes made in the Master Pages section will carry forward to every *new* use of that master page in the Pages section. If you've already edited a two-page spread in the Pages section, new changes to that master page in the Master Pages section will *not* carry forward to that page. If you haven't made any edits in the Pages section, though, they will.

(This is my conclusion based on trial and error. I know that sounds a little confusing, but basically if you make changes for the series or the template in the master pages and make changes for that specific title in the Pages section, you're probably going to be fine. Worst-case scenario, if the changes you make on a master page don't carry through to the Pages section and you need them to, then delete that page spread in the Pages section and add it again and they should.)

Okay. Next up is the copyright and chapter start master page.

COPYRIGHT AND CHAPTER START
MASTER PAGE

The copyright and chapter start master page is a little more complex because we're going to have text frames on both pages this time as well as adding a footer. What we want to end up with is this:

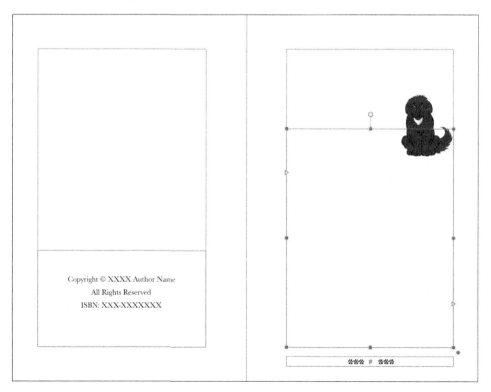

Copyright © XXXX Author Name
All Rights Reserved
ISBN: XXX-XXXXXXX

First step, go to the Master Pages section of the Pages studio and Duplicate the Title Page to create a new master page. Rename it Copyright and Chapter Start.

Left-click on that thumbnail in the Master Pages section and drag the master page to the end. You should see a blue line appear after the Also By master page, release when that happens and the Copyright master page should move to the bottom of the list of master pages.

(Note that you can minimize the Pages section if you want to by clicking on the little arrow next to Pages. That will let you see all of your master pages at once.)

Double-click on the thumbnail for the copyright master page to make sure it's the master page that's shown in your main workspace.

Now add a text frame on the left-hand side of the master page. (Frame Text Tool, click and drag. Align along the edges with the red and green lines.)

How big this text frame should be will depend on how much copyright language you want to include. I do the bare bones—just author name, all rights reserved, and the ISBN—so my text frame is small and at the bottom of the text area. If you did one more like a traditional publisher your text frame might need to be the entire text area.

Once you have the text frame, click on the Artistic Text Tool option (the A) on the left-hand side set of options, click into the text frame, and add your text. Format the text in your desired font.

I use 12 pt Baskerville URW centered. This is the same font and font size I will use for the main body text. You will likely not have that font available, but Garamond is a good choice and one you should have by default.

I highly recommend with any fiction title that you focus on one accent font for your chapter headers, book title page, etc. and one font for your main body text, copyright information, headers and footers, etc. So here I'm using Brushability Sans and Baskerville URW.

The font you choose for your chapter headers and title page can be more ornate or playful because it's only used as an accent. Ideally it should have multiple weights available and be a sans serif font, a decorative font, or a script font.

Brushability Sans is a sans serif font and has five different weights (Light, Regular, Semibold, Bold, and Black) available. The different weights give me a nice variety of choices for my different pages without requiring that I add a third font to my book. And the fact that it's a sans serif font keeps it from conflicting with my main body text which is a serifed font.

For your main body text you want a workhorse font that is easy to read. Unless you're doing large print or publishing for a specific audience with reading impairments, the font should be a serifed font because that's easier to read for most people. All of the Amazon templates use Garamond. Other good choices per IngramSpark are Caslon, Minion, and Palatino. Whatever font you choose, be sure you also have the italic version available because in Affinity you can only add italics if you have the italic version of a font.

If you have a book where you really loved the fonts sometimes they'll include a page at the back of the book that names the font.

You should be able to just type a c in parens—(c)—and it will automatically convert to the copyright symbol for you, but it doesn't work for me all of the time. (As I've been writing this book it's failed to work about 60% of the time, but has worked about 40% of the time.)

If it doesn't work for you, click where you want that symbol and then go to View-> Studio-> Glyph Browser to open the glyph browser studio.

If you've already applied your font that should be the font shown at the top. If it isn't, use the dropdown menu to choose the font you're going to use and then scroll down through the section that shows all of the letters and symbols in that font until you see the copyright symbol.

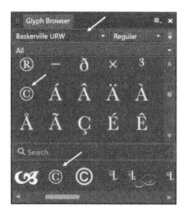

Double-click on it to add it to your document. It should appear at the point where you'd clicked into your document.

Once you've done that the first time the symbol should also be listed at the bottom of the glyph browser in your most recently used symbols section. You can double-click it from there as well.

Okay. Getting back to our master page. I entered and formatted my text and here's what I ended up with:

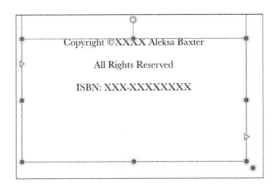

The X's are there to remind me that for each actual title I create I need to add the copyright year and ISBN.

Now, in the screenshot above that's the default spacing, but I want my lines of text to be closer together.

To fix that, I select the text, and go to the Paragraph studio in the top right of the workspace, click the checkbox for Space Between Same Styles, and then change the value there to 6 pt.

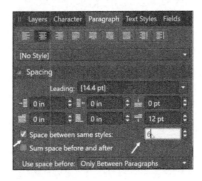

That brings each line of text closer together but not so close they're squished. I also want to change the size of that text frame to bring this text a little lower down on the page. I end up with this (keeping in mind that that line right above Copyright will not be visible on the page when I print this):

Next we need to put our chapter start on the right-hand side of the page.

In general, chapters in fiction books do not start at the top of the page. They usually start a certain amount of space lower. It'll be up to you where you want to set yours based on what "looks good", just be sure that it's enough space down the page to be a clear difference from being at the top of the page.

Also, keeping in mind that both your chapter headers (Chapter 1, Chapter 2, etc.) as well as your main body text will be in this text frame.

DO NOT try creating a separate text box for your chapter header, not unless you want to complicate your life in horrible ways. (Ask me how I know…)

I'm going to leave this one at a height of 4.75 which matches the title page. It'll create a smoother line for someone flipping through the book for those to be at the same height. That means I don't have to do anything to the text frame because it's already good to go.

Now that that's set, we're going to include our little dog image on the right-hand side and top of the text box. (You do not have to do this and for some it may seem like overkill to have an image at every chapter start, but just to show you what you could do with your chapter starts I'm going to do so.)

The image is already there, but I want to resize it because I want it a little smaller than it is on the title page.

Again, for consistency across pages, I'll use the same size as I did on the Also By page which was a height of 1.4. So I use the Transform studio to change the size of the image, making sure that the Lock Aspect Ratio option is checked.

I can then click and drag the image until it's aligned to the right-hand side of my text frame and centered along the top edge of the text frame for my chapter start. (I may decide to adjust that later if it doesn't look right with text added, but it's a good place to start.)

Finally, we need to add our footer to the bottom of the page.

Click on the Frame Text Tool (T) option and then click and drag to make a text frame that's located a little bit below the main text area. You want a text frame that is as wide as your main text frame and a little taller than the height of one line of the font that you're going to use in the main body of your document. (See the screenshot above for what I did.)

Next, click on the A, Artistic Text Tool, and click back into that text frame. Go to Text-> Insert -> Fields -> Page Number to insert a page number.

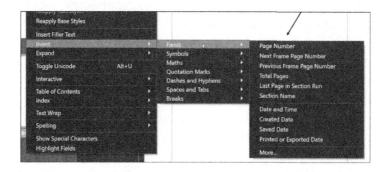

You should now see a # sign in that text frame. (In your actual document that will display as a number but in the master page it shows as a # sign.) Format it with the same font and font size as your main body text and center it.

(You can also choose to align away from spine instead of centering if you want, but I'm going to center. If you choose to align away from spine that will put your page numbers on the outer edge of each page. That option is available using the dropdown arrow at the end of the alignment options or at the top of the Paragraph studio.)

I also make sure to center the text in my footers vertically as well. To do that, use the top menu option to the right of where you center your text. It's a dropdown menu that is by default Top Aligned.

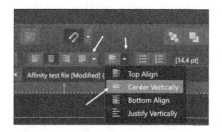

The reason I do that is because I had a book where I didn't do that and the book used images and for some reason that changed the alignment of my page numbers at the bottom of the page so that the page numbers where there were images on the page were lower than the page numbers where there weren't images.

If you want, you can also add images or flourishes around the page number as well.

Based on my experience, adding little flourishes that you can get from one of the fonts in the glyph browser is much easier than adding actual images to the document, but both are possible.

For this series I use a font called Ennobled Pet to put some paw prints on either side of my page number. I put three asterisks on either side and assign that font to it.

And here we are, a complete Copyright and Chapter Start page:

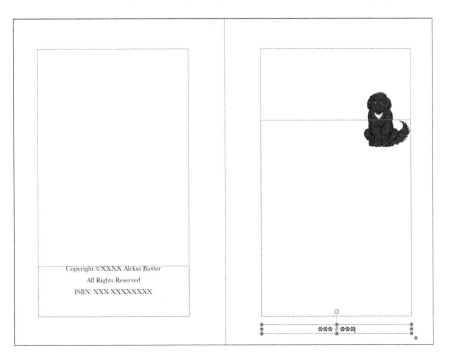

TEXT AND CHAPTER START MASTER PAGE

We're going to let that one sit for a minute while we create a couple more master pages.

Next one up is the Text and Chapter Start master page, which looks like this:

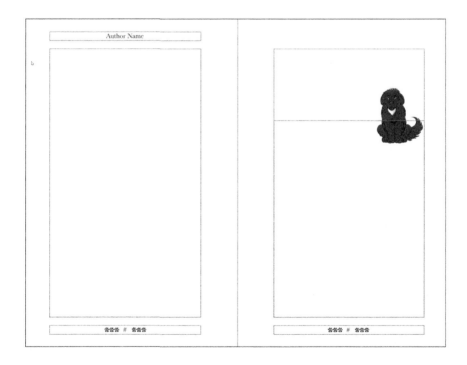

The easiest way to do this is to copy the Copyright and Chapter Start master page and then modify it.

So. Right-click, Duplicate, and then rename the new one. Double-click on the new one to make sure you're editing the right version.

The right-hand side of the master page is already done.

The first thing we need to do on the left-hand side is expand the text frame to fit the entire text space and then delete the copyright text. So, click on the text frame, use the blue circle to drag it to the top, then select the text in the frame and delete it.

Next, we need to add a header and footer to this page.

The footer is easy enough, you can just copy the footer from the right-hand page and drag that copy into place on the left-hand page.

You can do this a few ways. The first option is to go to the Layers studio, find the page number layer, right-click, Duplicate, then go to the workspace and click on the page number layer and drag it to the left.

A second option is to click on the Move Tool and then click on the footer in the workspace, Ctrl + C and then Ctrl+ V to copy and paste, and then left-click and drag the copy to its new location on the left-hand page.

With both options, make sure that when you click and drag your new footer aligns with the old footer as well as the text area on the left-hand page. Like so:

If for some reason the snapping lines aren't appearing, try clicking on your footer layers in the Layers panel first. Or you can just take the Y value from the Transform studio for the original footer and use the same Y value for the new one.

Now we need our header. Copy the footer and move it to the top.

It's easy enough to align it with your active text space but a little trickier to place it at the same distance from the main text frame as you placed your footer. To do that, click on the footer and arrow up and then down to see the numeric value that is shown next to the blue arrowed line drawn between the main text frame and the footer text frame.

You can then click on the header text frame and arrow up or down until you get the same value between the header text frame and main text frame. In my case I was able to get within .01 of the same value which should be visually about the same to a reader.

After the header is in place, you need to delete the text that's currently in there and then replace it with the header information. In fiction books you generally have the author name on the left-hand page and the book title on the right-hand page. Affinity lets you use fields to add both of these, but we need to set those field values up first for it to work.

To do so, go to the Fields studio which should be on the right-hand top side. Click into the space next to Author and add your author name. And then click into the space next to Title and add your book title.

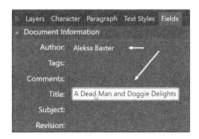

Now click into the header text frame, delete the text that's there, and add your Author field.

To do that, go to the Fields studio and double-click on Author on the left-hand side. (So not the Author Name you typed in on the right-hand side, but the label.) This will insert the *value* you have listed for Author into that text frame, not the field name.

(If you used a special font to add accents to your footers like I had, you may then need to change the font to your chosen main body font.)

If the Fields studio isn't open or you can't find it, you can go to Text-> Insert-> Fields and then choose More from the dropdown. That will open the Fields studio for you.

And that's it. There you have it. A master page for when there's text on the left-hand side of the page and a chapter start on the right-hand side of the page.

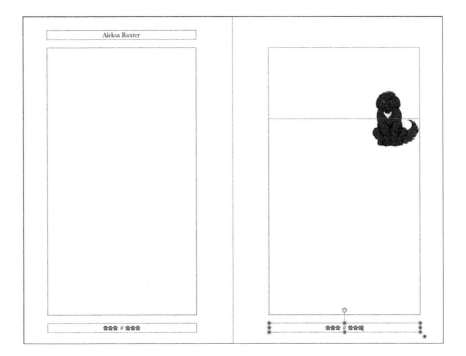

Okay, now the Text and Text master page and then we can start creating the beginning of our book.

TEXT AND TEXT MASTER PAGE

The Text and Text master page is for those portions of the book where there's just text on both sides of the page. It looks like this:

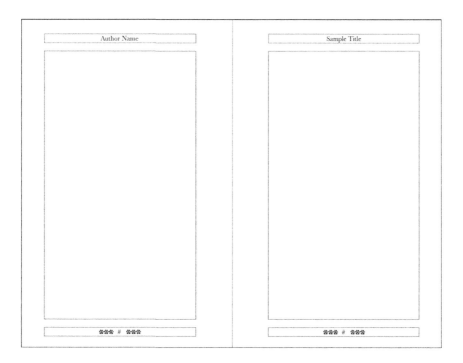

To create the Text and Text master page, duplicate the Text and Chapter Start master page you just created and rename it. Be sure to double-click on the renamed master page so that you're editing the right one. (I say this multiple times because it's a mistake I make often and then I have to change the names around.)

Okay. We already have the left-hand side done. We just need to fix the right-hand side.

So. Delete the image. Be sure you have the Move Tool selected if you want to click on the image in the workspace itself, otherwise go to the Layers studio and click on the layer with the image in it and then hit the Delete key.

Next, resize the text box for that side so that it covers the entire text area.

After that, copy the header from the left-hand page over to the right-hand page. You can do that in the Layers panel or right-click, Copy, Paste in the workspace itself. Click and drag so that your header on your right-hand page is aligned with your header on the left-hand page as well as the text area for the right-hand page.

Now click on the A for the Artistic Text Tool. Go back to that header on the right-hand page and delete the Author name. Replace it with the field for Title by going to the Fields studio and double-clicking on Title. Note that Affinity will insert your value for that field not the field name.

You should now have a master page spread with your author name in the header on the left, your title in the header on the right, page numbers in the footers, and two text frames that are the size of the designated text area:

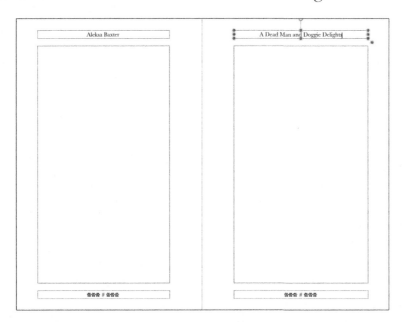

Done.

BUILD THE BEGINNING OF YOUR DOCUMENT

So far your actual document has a title page and an also by page. We now need to add two more page spreads to that document. To do so, go to the Pages section. (If you minimized it, it will be at the bottom of the Pages studio.)

Click on the also by page spreads, Pages 2, 3. Right-click. Choose Add Pages from the dropdown.

In the Add Pages dialogue box you want 2 pages, After, Page 3, and Copyright and Chapter Start for the master page. OK.

Next, right-click on that newly-added page spread, Pages 4, 5, which should be the Copyright and Chapter Start pages, and choose Add Pages again.

This time it's 2 pages, After, Page 5, and the dropdown option you want is Text and Text.

That should give you a document with seven pages.

The first is your title page, followed by a blank page and Also By, followed by a copyright page and your first chapter start, followed by two pages for just text that have a header and footer.

It should look like the screenshot on the next page.

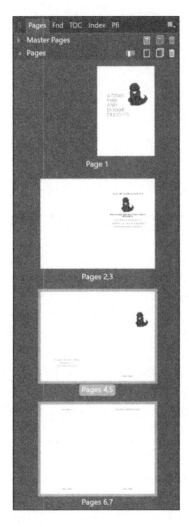

Alright, now that that's done, we're almost ready to add our main document text, but one thing we haven't addressed yet is text flow between frames. Let's do that next.

TEXT FLOW BETWEEN FRAMES

One of the wonders of Affinity (or probably any professional print design program) is that you can have your text flow from one text frame to the next automatically. The key though is that you have to link them so that Affinity knows you want that to happen.

To do so, go to the Master Pages section and open the Text and Text master page by double-clicking on it.

You should have two text frames, one on each page. The problem is, we haven't linked them yet. So any text I paste into that left-hand text frame will stay in that left-hand text frame. And any text I paste into that right-hand text frame will stay in that right-hand text frame.

But what I want is for the text in the left-hand frame to flow to the right-hand frame once the left-hand frame fills up.

To make that happen, we need to tell Affinity to continue any additional text from the left-hand main text frame into the right-hand main text frame.

It's very easy to do.

First, click on the text frame on the left-hand side. When you do this, you should see that the text frame has an outline and that there are little blue arrows visible on the left and right edges of the text frame.

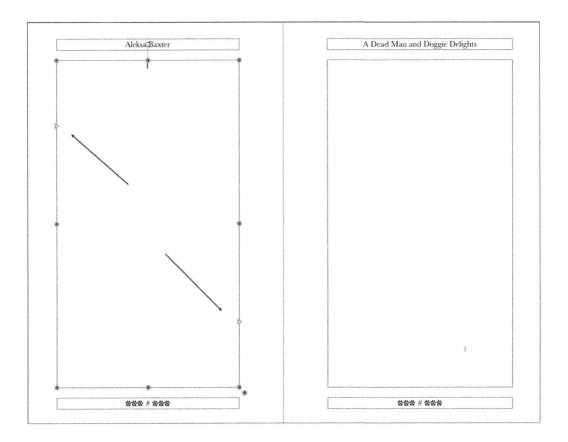

Click on the blue arrow on the right-hand edge of that left-hand text frame and then click into the text frame on the right-hand page. Before your click on the right-hand text frame it will be shaded in blue like this to show you where the text will flow to:

After you click on that right-hand text frame that will disappear, but you should now see a line that connects the two text frames.

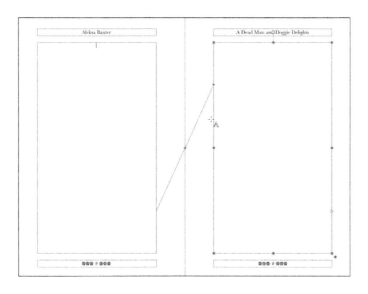

That line tells you that when there is too much text to fit in the left-hand frame, it will flow to the right-hand frame. It will *follow* that line in the direction of that arrow. (This is important to keep in mind in case you ever get that reversed. I once tried to create a master page by copying an existing master page and swapping the text frames that were already linked and it reversed the flow of the text so that it went right-to-left. So the direction of those arrows matters.)

For each master page that you create that has more than one main text frame you need to tell Affinity to flow the text between the frames. That means right now we also need to do this for the Text and Chapter Start master page. Go and do that. It's the same process. Click on the blue arrow on the right edge of the left-hand text frame and then click on the right-hand text frame.

(I probably should have had you do it when we created the templates, but this is the order in which my mind thinks of these things and as long as you get them all into place by the end, you're fine.)

That's text flow between text frames within master pages, but we also need to tell Affinity to flow text between our two main body master pages that we just added, pages 4, 5 and 6, 7 in the Pages section.

To do so, double-click on the Pages 4, 5 thumbnail in the Pages section. Then in the main workspace scroll down a bit until you can see the bottom of Pages 4, 5 and the top of Pages 6, 7.

Now, click on the text frame on the right-hand page for Pages 4, 5 (the top of the two spreads that you can see). Then click on that blue arrow on the right edge of the frame. Next, click on the main text frame on the left-hand side for Pages 6, 7 (the bottom of the two spreads that you can see). It should look like this when you're done, with a blue line connecting Page 5 to Page 6:

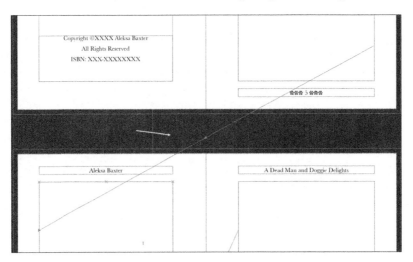

This tells Affinity to take text from that chapter start master page and flow it down to the text and text master page that comes next.

Okay. We basically have everything in place at the moment to bring in our main document text. Once we do that, we'll talk about text styles.

It doesn't feel like it, but with this groundwork we've laid we are probably 75% of the way there right now because Affinity is about to do a lot of the heavy lifting for us.

ADD YOUR MAIN BODY TEXT

At this point you're going to ignore the Master Pages section of the Pages studio for the time being. Minimize it. Put it away. Click on that little arrow next to Master Pages and let's focus in on our Pages section and the document we want to create.

(We will be going back to it later because there are more master pages we still need to create, but for now let's move on to something more interesting.)

Okay. Double-click on the thumbnail for the pages that have your first chapter start. For me that's pages 4, 5. You should now see both of those pages in your main workspace.

If for some reason you can't easily see both pages in your view, go to View-> Zoom and then Zoom to Fit or Zoom to Width. One of those two should work so that you can see both pages of the spread in your workspace at the same time. Usually I run into this visibility issue when I move from the Master Page section to the Pages section, I don't know why.

Now, go to wherever you have the main body text of your document stored and copy that text. You don't want your front matter or back matter, but you do want all of the chapters. All of them. Chapter headers and text.

So, Ctrl + A to select all, Ctrl + C to copy, at least in Word.

Next, click into the main text frame where your first chapter is supposed to start and use Ctrl + V to paste your text.

If you can't click into the text box, be sure you've clicked on the A on the left-hand side first to activate the Artistic Text Tool.

You should see something like this.

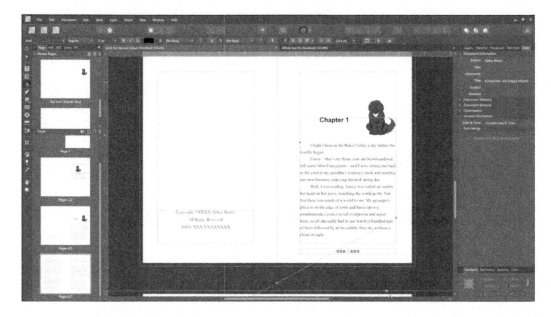

Because we already told Affinity to flow the text from this page to the next, it does. We have three pages of text and the beginning of a novel.

But you can't see more text than that even though we pasted in more than a hundred pages of text because there are no more pages for the text to flow to. It's in the document right now, just not visible.

And you can tell that there's more text hiding, because on the right-edge of that chapter start page and where there's normally a blue circle, it's now red. Scroll down to the next two pages and you'll see more red circles and possibly a red arrow on the right-hand edge of the last main text frame there on page 7.

That's because we pasted in more text than there was space for and those red marks are Affinity telling you that.

This is a key thing to understand about Affinity if you're used to working in Word like I am. Because in Word you usually see all of your text. But in Affinity you can have text that isn't visible because Affinity will only display text in your text frames and if there aren't enough of them it just doesn't display that text. But the text is still there.

I'm hitting on this one hard, because I get caught out by this on a somewhat regular basis.

For example, I will delete all of the pages of a two hundred page document and think that's all I needed to do because I no longer see that text. But behind the scenes Affinity still has the text that was in those two hundred pages.

So I always have to remind myself to delete the text first. And then I can delete the pages, too.

Sometimes this pops up when I go to create a table of contents and it puts in an about the author section, for example, that I didn't realize was still there. So if that ever happens to you, that's why.

Okay. Putting that aside, right now we have three pages of our main document and about two hundred pages of text that's there but you can't see.

It's time to tell Affinity to add enough pages and flow that remaining text to make it all visible.

To do this, go to the right-hand main text frame of the Text and Text page spread on pages 6,7, so the frame on page 7.

If you see a red circle along the right-hand edge, click on it. It should turn into a red arrow. Otherwise you should see the red arrow and a little eye with a slash through it that looks like this:

> With a shotgun.
>
> There I was, hanging onto the fence, Fancy barking her head off at my feet, and my grandpa comes walking around the side of the house to confront the guy, shotgun in hand. At least I was pretty sure it was a

What you want to do is hold down the Shift key and click on that red arrow on the right-hand edge of the right-most text frame.

If you do this right, Affinity should start adding pages for you and flowing your text to those new pages.

The reason I had you add a Text and Text master page as the last page spread in our document is because Affinity adds pages using whatever master page spread you were using on that last page. Since the bulk of the pages in a novel are text and text, having Affinity use that master page spread to add our pages saves us the most effort because it's already applying our most frequently-used master page spread for us.

So here we go. With just that shift and click I suddenly have a document with 239 pages of text all placed neatly in my text frames and flowing from one page to the next.

Isn't that awesome? Think how much time and energy that just saved us. No inserting master pages, no linking text frames. All of it already done for us.

Okay. Now we need to put in place our text styles to save even more time and energy.

TEXT STYLES

A text style is a shortcut that allows you to apply formatting to your text in a quick and easy way. Once you set up one you never have to go through the process of choosing your font, font weight, font size, paragraph and character formatting, etc. again to get that specific appearance. You can just apply the text style.

Even better, you can assign keyboard shortcuts to your text styles which can save a ton of time when formatting the main body of your document. I usually have text styles and shortcuts assigned to my chapter headers, my first paragraph, and my main body text. That lets me quickly move through my entire document and apply formatting to the text as needed.

Sometimes for non-fiction I also have a text style and shortcut assigned to subheaders as well.

FIRST PARAGRAPH TEXT STYLE

Okay. So how do we set a text style up?

It's pretty easy. We'll start with the first paragraph text style.

Go to your first page of the main body of your document. This is Chapter 1 for most of us and should be Page 5 if you've been following along and building a document according to what I've listed out here.

Click on the Artistic Text Tool and then highlight your first paragraph.

Now choose all of the formatting you want for that paragraph from the top menu options. For me that's going to be Baskerville URW, Regular, 12 pt, Align Left.

(In the actual books I've published for this series I used Justify Left instead. Those are the two common choices you have for paragraph formatting.)

Next, go to the Paragraph studio and set your Leading to the desired value. I usually use Default which in this case shows as 14.4. And because this is a first paragraph and I don't want it indented, I also need to go to the second option on the left-hand side of the Spacing section and set the First Line Indent value to 0.

Once the paragraph looks the way you want it to, it's time to save this formatting as a Text Style.

In the top menu next to the Paragraph mark, you should see a dropdown that currently reads [No Style]. Be careful, because there may be two of them and you want the second one. Click on that dropdown arrow and the second option should be New Style.

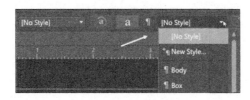

Click on that. This will open the Create Paragraph Style dialogue box which looks like this:

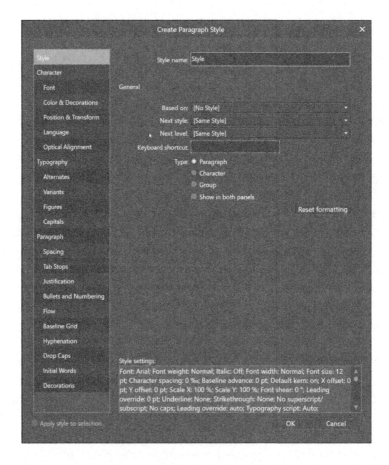

If there aren't that many options on the left-hand side, you probably went to the wrong dropdown and opened the Create Character Style dialogue box instead. If so, close and use the other dropdown menu.

First things first, in the Style Name box, type in the name you want to use for this style. Make it something descriptive that you can immediately identify. I like to use First Paragraph for my first paragraph style.

At this point, because we already formatted the paragraph in our document, it's ready to go and we could just click on OK and be done right now. But while we're here, let's add a keyboard shortcut for this one.

I like to use Shift + 1 for Chapter Heading, Shift + 2 for First Paragraph, and Shift + 3 for Main Body text. Having them in order like that makes it easy for me to just go through in my head which one I need. (I sometimes use the wrong one still as you'll see in the videos, but that's an easy enough fix.) And they are also easy to reach when I'm typing.

I don't necessarily recommend using the same shortcut keys I do. Because if you think about it for a second, you'll realize that those are also the exclamation mark, at sign, and pound sign. For me it works because what I'm doing in Affinity is 99% formatting. If I were also typing a lot of text in Affinity I'd run into an issue where instead of, for example, getting an exclamation mark as planned, I reformatted a paragraph.

It doesn't happen to me often enough for me to change that up, although I do run into this problem with my books on Excel where I use Shift + 4 for subheaders and also need to make a few edits that involve the $ sign.

Okay. So pick the key combination you want for your keyboard shortcut for your first paragraph. Mine is going to be Shift + 2.

Go to the Keyboard Shortcut field and type the shortcut. So, for me, I'd hold down the Shift key and type 2. Affinity will interpret what you type and place a description of what you typed into the text box for you.

Once that's done you can click on OK and you have a First Paragraph text style that can be applied using your keyboard shortcut.

MAIN BODY TEXT STYLE

In an ideal world, your text styles would be nested, meaning that you have one primary text style that uses your main body font and you have another primary text style that uses your accent font. Any other text styles that use those same fonts would be secondary to the primary text styles. This way, if you wanted to change your font from say, Baskerville URW to Garamond, you could do so by editing just one text style.

Sounds confusing, I know. But in execution it's much easier. So let's do that now with our main body text.

What I want you to do is go to the second paragraph in that first chapter, which should be your first main body paragraph. And I want you to apply the first paragraph text style to it. So Shift + 2 for me.

If you didn't have a keyboard shortcut set up you could choose the style from the dropdown menu in the top section or you could go to the Text Styles studio and choose it from there.

Now that we have this paragraph formatted as a First Paragraph we can edit it to be a main body paragraph. The only difference for me between the first paragraph and the main body paragraph is the paragraph indent.

So I go to the Paragraph studio, go to the Spacing section, and change the value for the second option on the left-hand side (First Line Indent) to .2.

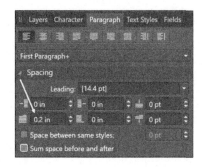

My paragraph is no longer using the First Paragraph style. And if you look at the dropdown menu up top for text style you will see that it shows as First Paragraph+. That is telling you that you started with the First Paragraph text style, but have made edits to it.

If you are ever trying to update a text style and want that text style to now use your updates, you can do so by clicking on the paragraph mark with a swoosh to the right of that dropdown menu.

It will only be an available option if you have in some way changed the formatting of that paragraph. But that is NOT what we want right now. We want to create a new style based on the old one.

So click on the dropdown arrow next to the style name, go to the top of the dropdown using the bar on the right-hand side, and choose New Style again.

This will open the Create Paragraph Style dialogue box once more.

Type in the name you want for the style in the Style Name box. I'm going to use Body Text. Also add your keyboard shortcut. I'm using Shift + 3.

And note what it looks like at the bottom for the style settings description.

It's basically saying, "Whatever that first paragraph does, do that, and then indent the line by this much."

Which is great when you want to change out the font or the font size for the entire novel. Right? You just update the First Paragraph style and this one will update as well.

That can also be dangerous, though, if you forget that you have your styles linked in this way and you try changing one style and forget that it will impact all of the others.

So you need to give a little thought to which of your styles you use for that primary style.

I have in the past (because I do make all the mistakes at some point in time) made a header and footer style my primary and linked a section header style as secondary and then forgotten. When I did it they were both centered and that was fine. But then I changed the header and footer style to be aligned to outer edge of the page and that automatically changed the section header to be the same, which did not work.

Just be careful and think it through. And be sure that your last step with any book you format is to look through the entire book, page by page, and make sure that everything looks good.

Click OK and you have your second style. We just need one more for our chapter headings.

CHAPTER HEADING TEXT STYLE

Highlight your first chapter heading or title. For me that's Chapter 1.

Now apply the formatting you want for that heading.

I'm going to stick with Brushability Sans, in a SemiBold weight and 20 pt size. I want it left-aligned because I have that image there on the right-hand side.

I also want some space before the first line of text.

If you are ever tempted to create distance between lines of text using an Enter, stop. There is a paragraph formatting option that will do that for you and will always keep things consistent. You do not want extra Enters anywhere in your document. What you want is to add a value for Space After Paragraph. In this case, 12 pt. It's found in the Paragraph studio on the right-hand side of the Spacing section.

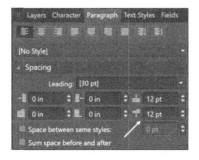

Once your formatting is set, go to the dropdown, click on New Style, name your style, assign your keyboard shortcut (mine for this is Shift + 1), and click OK.

This style is one that should not be based on your first paragraph or body text styles because it uses the accent font, but it can be a good one to base all of your front matter styles off of if you want to create styles for those.

APPLY MAIN BODY TEXT STYLE TO ALL

We now have the three primary text styles that we need for the main body of the book.

If we had also used styles in Word or wherever we copied our text from and Affinity had carried over those style names (which it does sometimes) we could now do a find and replace for each paragraph style and be done with assigning those text styles.

But since I used an RTF file from Vellum which does not carry over, I now have to apply those styles manually.

Since body text is going to be the majority of the text in this book, I use Ctrl + A to select all of the text I pasted into the main body and then Shift + 3 to apply the Body Text style format to everything. (It won't impact my front matter, because those pages are not linked to these text frames.)

By doing that I did erase the pretty formatting I put in place for my chapter start and my first paragraph, but that's easy enough to solve. I click on the line with Chapter 1 and use Shift + 1 and then I click on the line below that for my first paragraph and use Shift +2. And this is what I have for the first page:

CHAPTER 1

I hadn't been in the Baker Valley a day before the trouble began.

Fancy—that's my three-year-old Newfoundland, full name Miss Fancypants—and I were sitting out back in the yard at my grandpa's reading a book and minding our own business, enjoying the mid-spring day.

Well, I was reading. Fancy was curled up nearby, her head on her paws, watching the world go by. Not that there was much of a world to see. My grandpa's place is on the edge of town and backs up to a mountainside covered in tall evergreens and aspen trees, so all she really had to see was five hundred feet of trees followed by an incredibly blue sky without a cloud in sight.

Man, I love Colorado.

Anyway. There we were, minding our own business, not bothering a soul, when Fancy jumped up and raced to the fence, barking like a mad woman. And it wasn't her "Hey, is that a dog, can we play?" bark either. It was her, "There's a jerk too close to my home" bark.

I reluctantly set my book aside—I'd just gotten to the good part, too—and dragged myself over to see what

It looks like it should in terms of paragraph and chapter heading formats.

ASSESS YOUR APPEARANCE

Now that you've created a first chapter master page and dropped in your text, it's time to stop and assess your document's appearance.

Look at that first page.

Does it look good to you?

Do you like where the image is relative to the text and chapter header? Do you like the amount of space between the chapter header and the first line of text? Do you like the fonts you're using? Do you like where the chapter starts on the page? Should it be higher? Should it be lower?

What about the justification you're using? Do you like having a ragged right margin if that's what you have? Do you like having the paragraphs justified if that's what you went with? Should you hyphenate your words to make it look better?

(To change justification go to the top menu or the Paragraph studio. To add hyphenation go to the Paragraph studio, Hyphenation section, and click Use Auto-Hyphenation.)

What about line spacing? Is there enough space between lines but not too much? What about the main body indent? Did you indent enough but not too much?

Basically, is this how you want your book to look?

Because if you change your mind later it's going to be a lot of redone work to go back and do the next steps again. So right now is the time to make these decisions. If that image needs to move, go fix it on the master page right now. If that chapter header needs to be bigger or smaller or have a bigger space from the text, fix it now.

Anything that's nagging at you, fix.

For example, I think I want that image to be up a bit, more in line with my chapter header than centered on that line. So I'm going to make that change in the two master pages I have that contain that image right now.

If you do move that image, use the Transform studio to make sure that the image is at the same height (Y) on both pages.

Yep. I like this much better.

CHAPTER 1

I hadn't been in the Baker Valley a day before the trouble began.

Fancy—that's my three-year-old Newfoundland, full name Miss Fancypants—and I were sitting out back in the yard at my grandpa's reading a book and minding our own business, enjoying the mid-spring day.

Well, I was reading. Fancy was curled up nearby, her head on her paws, watching the world go by. Not that there was much of a world to see. My grandpa's place is on the edge of town and backs up to a mountainside covered in tall evergreens and aspen trees, so all she really had to see was five hundred feet of trees followed by an incredibly blue sky without a cloud in sight.

Man, I love Colorado.

Anyway. There we were, minding our own business, not bothering a soul, when Fancy jumped up and raced to the fence, barking like a mad woman. And it wasn't her "Hey, is that a dog, can we play?" bark either. It was her, "There's a jerk too close to my home" bark.

I reluctantly set my book aside—I'd just gotten to the good part, too—and dragged myself over to see what

By fixing this now I avoid a lot of extra, unnecessary work. Normally I'd probably justify my paragraphs as well, but I'm going to leave them as is.

* * *

There's also one other choice you need to make that you can't see so much right now. That's how to handle widows and orphans. These are single lines that appear at the top or bottom of the page that are part of a paragraph but have been separated from it. You're really not supposed to have them if you can avoid it.

Now is the time to decide whether you want Affinity to automatically remove them for you, which may result in the text on facing pages ending at different points on the page, or whether you'll try to fix them manually. I fix mine by hand because I like my text to line up at the bottom of the page.

If you want Affinity to do that for you (and I do have Affinity do it for large print where that matters more), then go to the Paragraph studio, Flow Options section, and check the boxes to prevent them.

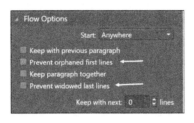

* * *

Finalize your overall appearance now. Because from here on out we are going to be fixing little fiddly issues and assigning master pages based upon where your text falls on the page and that is driven by all of these decisions.

SECTION BREAKS

Next up, it's time to figure out what you want to do about section breaks, because in a lot of instances you can handle them all at once with a find and replace.

I once made the mistake of using an image for a section break and that was time-consuming and annoying because I had issues getting it to center for me which meant I had to place each one individually and click and drag it around to get it where I needed it.

Ever since then I've stuck to fonts or glyphs that are available in my glyph browser.

For example, for my cozy mysteries I use the Ennobled Pet font. It turns an asterisk into a cute little dog paw print.

The full formatting I use is that font, 12 pt, with 6 pt spacing above and below, and centered. Because I'm basically using * * * as my section divider and I don't use that anywhere else, I can easily do a find and replace throughout the whole document and update my section breaks all at once.

(I do need to keep in mind when I do this that I still want to apply the first paragraph text style to each paragraph that follows a section break, but at least it saves a little effort.)

And don't think that there aren't some good possibilities using text only. For example in my fantasy series I was able to use moons and stars for the section breaks because one of the Wingdings fonts includes them. I also have fonts I've bought that come with a separate embellishment version that has all sorts of little lines and shapes to use. So you can still get creative with your section breaks without that much effort.

So how do we apply a style to all of our breaks at once?

You're going to use the Find and Replace studio. If you set your workspace up like mine it will be the second tab on the left-hand side. Find pretty much works like in any standard program. Type your text in below where it says Find and then click on the Find option to show your results.

It will give a listing of all results for that symbol, word, or phrase. Click on each one to go to that page in your document.

So in this case, I would search for * * *, click on Find, and then click on the first result it gave me.

In my workspace, that section break is now highlighted and I can format it however I want and then create a new text style for it. I'm going to creatively name mine Section Break.

Once you've done that, you can go back to the Find and Replace studio and in the Replace section add the text you used for your revised section break (for me that's still * * *) and then click on the little gear symbol off to the right-hand side, go down to Paragraph Style, and choose your Section Break paragraph style.

(I will note here that there have been times when I tried to search for a style that should have been there in that list and it wasn't. So this isn't 100% but it works most of the time.)

You should now see your paragraph style name directly below the replace field. Like this:

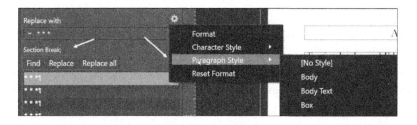

Once you have everything set, click on Replace All and Affinity will replace all of your initial section breaks with the new one formatted the way you wanted using your section break style.

You should then be able to click on the search results to navigate through the document and see that all of your section breaks are now formatted the way you wanted. If you really want to, you can update each paragraph after your breaks to use the first paragraph style as you do so. (I am generally not that efficient, but it would be a smart thing to do.)

FIND AND REPLACE
FOR CHAPTER HEADINGS

If you really wanted to get fancy with saving time, you could also use find and replace for your chapter headings, assuming they are listed as Chapter 1, Chapter 2, etc.

Because the text style we assigned to chapter headings is for the whole "paragraph" you can do a find and replace for the word Chapter that replaces it with the word Chapter and assigns the Chapter Header text style.

If you do that, the whole line will be assigned that text style. So even though you only searched for Chapter and not Chapter 1, both words will get the new format.

Obviously this doesn't work if you just used numbers and not the word "chapter." It also doesn't work if you name your chapters.

And keep in mind that any paragraph that includes the word "chapter" is going to get that formatting as well and you'll have to fix it.

I don't normally do this, but it could save time if you wanted to.

THE MAIN BODY OF YOUR DOCUMENT

Now that everything looks the way you want it to, you're ready to start walking through the document and applying master pages, text styles, and fixing any issues with your text such as orphans, widows, too short a word ending a paragraph, a chapter ending with a single line or two on a page, and any other errors or issues that look "wrong".

To do this, start at your first page and work your way forward. You have to do this in order because every fix you apply to an earlier page can impact the fix you need to apply to a later page.

For example, if I apply a chapter start master page that pushes the text on that page down to account for where the chapter heading starts and to make room for the chapter heading, that then impacts which lines of text are at the top and bottom of the next page.

So I don't want to fix an orphan on page 25 if I haven't assigned the chapter start master page on page 20. That orphan may no longer exist once the appropriate master pages have been applied.

And I don't want to apply a master page for a chapter start on page 100 if I haven't fixed a prior chapter that ends with just one line of text on the page, because once I do that, page 100 will no longer be where that chapter starts.

You have to work your way through from the first page to the last. And if you make any big universal formatting changes (like your font, font size, line spacing, etc.) then you have to go back to that first page and start again. That's why we did that assessment earlier. Because you don't want to have to redo all this work. So get it right before you start.

Now let's walk through everything you're going to do.

APPLY TEXT STYLES

Applying text styles is easy if you set it up like I did.

For each chapter start, Shift + 1. For each first paragraph of a chapter or section, Shift + 2. And you shouldn't actually have to use Shift + 3 because we already formatted all of our text with it. But just in case, it's there to use. (For example, if you used find and replace for chapter headings and it turns out you had a paragraph that contained the word chapter.)

Applying master pages, takes a little more effort. Let's talk about that next.

APPLY MASTER PAGES

Here I have the start of Chapter 2. It's nice and easy to see because the text from Chapter 1 ends fairly high up on the prior page.

complications that might delay the opening that that was Jamie-speak for all hell had broken loose. I needed to see just how bad things were.

As I pulled out of the driveway I figured at least it wasn't going to be worse than my grandpa pointing a shotgun at someone, right?

Wrong.

Chapter 2

By the time I reached the store I'd calmed down enough to see the humor in the whole shotgun situation. It helped that I had a good twenty minute drive to get there. And not through urban sprawl like I was used to, but along a two-lane highway that wound its way through cattle land that was green with spring and dotted with the occasional red barn or one-story ranch home tucked away half a mile off the highway, usually down some rutted dirt road separated from the rest of the world by a rusted metal gate.

The whole area is called Baker Valley because it's a long narrow valley tucked into the Colorado mountains. For tourist trap purposes the towns in the area all agreed to pool their advertising funds and advertise the whole valley, but there are actually a half dozen small towns spread throughout the area. My grandpa's place is at the west end of the valley in a town creatively named Creek that has two gas stations, one church, the county seat, a funeral home, a pioneer museum, and about forty houses, half of which probably started off as mobile homes until someone built a foundation around them.

About ten minutes from there is the town of Masonville. It's where everyone in the valley goes to school and boasts its own McDonald's and a supermarket. (New additions in the last decade. Prior to that folks would drive the hour and half into Denver to stock up on groceries once a month, assuming they didn't live on the deer they hunted and the vegetables they grew in their backyard.)

Another ten minutes past Masonville is the shining

Because this is the beginning of Chapter 2, I need a different master page than Text and Text. I need the Text and Chapter Start master page here.

The way to do that is to find the thumbnail of this page in the Pages section of the Pages studio on the left-hand side. Click on it so that the full thumbnail is selected.

It should be fairly obvious which one it is because of where the text ends on the left-hand page. (When it isn't that obvious I will sometimes format my chapter header first to make it more obvious.)

You can also use the page numbers to find the correct spread. Because I haven't yet had you change the page numbering for this section of the document—something you will need to do—the page numbers you see in the main workspace should still match those in the Pages section, so that's another option as well.

So find the page spread you need to change, right-click on the thumbnail in the Pages section, and choose Apply Master from the dropdown menu.

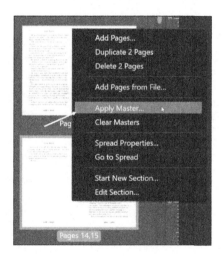

This will bring up the Apply Master dialogue box:

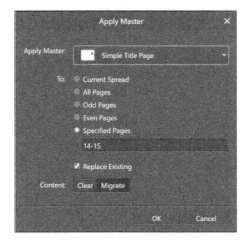

Click on the dropdown arrow next to the first master page name at the top of the dialogue box and choose the master page you want to apply. In this case Text and Chapter Start. Then click OK.

(This is why I like to order my master pages. Because once you have a decent number of them it makes it easier to find the one you want if they're in an intuitive order. For others, moving them to be alphabetical might work better. And some may just enjoy the chaos of leaving them as is.)

Here's that same two-page spread with the new master page applied. All I did was apply the master page, I didn't have to move the text down the page or anything like that. Applying the master page did that for me.

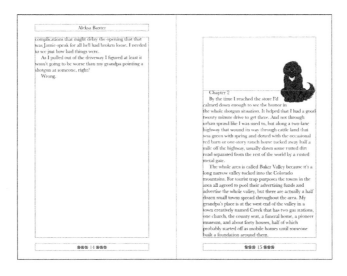

See how it added in our image and dropped the text down to where we want a chapter to start? Now all you need to do is apply the chapter heading style (Shift + 1) and the first paragraph style (Shift + 2) and this page is good to go.

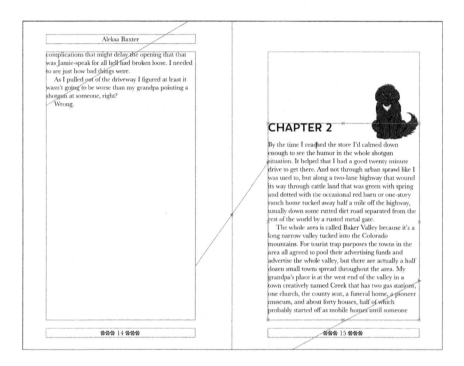

Although, that did create a widowed last line that continues onto the next page. So let's talk about strategies for manually fixing widows and orphans next.

MANUALLY FIX WIDOWS AND ORPHANS

If you chose not to have Affinity automatically fix your widows and orphans then you're going to need to fix them manually yourself. That's what I prefer to do because it gives me more control and lets my text be level at the bottom of each page.

The way I try to remove widows and orphans is by adjusting the tracking on that paragraph or surrounding paragraphs that will impact the one I'm trying to fix.

Tracking is located in the Positioning and Transform section of the Character studio. It is the second option on the left-hand side with an arrowed line under the letters VA.

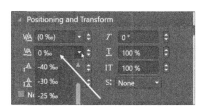

There is a dropdown there and what I generally do is try to tighten up a paragraph enough to bring the text in that paragraph up one line.

I try not to take this value past about -20% or so. I don't want the difference in the spacing to be noticeable to my readers. But if you're using justified text sometimes there can be big jumps because of a large word that was hanging up the paragraph so -25% can sometimes look better than -20%.

Let me show you an example. Here I have a two-page spread where there is the end of a paragraph stranded at the top of the page:

Aleksa Baxter

was bothering her. She'll usually stop if I just check out whatever it is and tell her she's been a good girl, but as I was walking across the yard I heard someone barking back at her.

That's right. Some jerk on the other side of the fence was barking at my dog. Seriously? I mean, what the…? Who does that?

I'd just spent five years living in Washington, DC and not once had someone barked at my dog. They'd stepped away from her like she had the plague, and there'd been an inordinate number of people who thought leaving chicken bones on the sidewalk was just fine and dandy, but none of them had barked at my dog.

And, because I was still in big city mode and not "love thy neighbor because you live in a town of a hundred where everyone knows everyone" mode, I stepped up on that little board along the bottom of the fence and told the guy off.

You know what he did? You know what that jerk did then?

He barked at me, too!

He lunged at me like he was going to attack me and barked. Three times. Woof, woof, woof.

I just stared at him like he was crazy. I mean, I'd moved to Baker Valley because it was supposed to be peaceful and nice and this is what I got on my first full day there? Some weird man barking at me? I didn't even know what to do at that point.

Unfortunately, while I was busy trying to figure out if werewolves might actually be real, which would at least explain the man's ridiculous behavior, my grandpa

❀❀❀ 6 ❀❀❀

A Dead Man and Doggie Delights

got involved.

With a shotgun.

There I was, hanging onto the fence, Fancy barking her head off at my feet, and my grandpa comes walking around the side of the house to confront the guy, shotgun in hand. At least I was pretty sure it was a shotgun, I'm not a gun person myself, but it had two long barrels that he pointed right at the guy. After cocking it or whatever it is you do with a shotgun to let someone know that when you pull that trigger it's gonna hurt.

"Son, you'd best get on your way." He planted his feet and pointed the gun right at the man, steady as steady could be.

I held my breath wondering if the man was stupid enough to bark at him, too. I figured it was a fifty-fifty chance and I really didn't know what my grandpa would do at that point, but I was pretty sure I didn't want to find out.

Fortunately, the guy just backed away, hands up. "Sorry, Mr. Carver. Didn't mean any offense. Just walking by."

"Well walk a little faster." My grandpa followed him with the gun, eyes flinty and jaw clenched tight. "And next time you leave my granddaughter alone or I'll put you in the ground where you belong, you hear me?"

"Grandpa," I hissed. "You can't say things like that."

This was exactly the type of thing I'd moved to Baker Valley to prevent. Well, okay, I'd had no idea before I moved that my grandpa was capable of pointing a gun at someone and threatening to put them in the ground where they belonged, but he had been

❀❀❀ 7 ❀❀❀

If I look back to the page before that line, I can see that I have two paragraphs on that prior page that end with short words.

One paragraph ends with just "dog." and one ends with just "then?" Both are good candidates for fixing this issue. (And honestly I might want to fix them just because ending a paragraph with a three-letter word is borderline bad formatting. Two-letter word, definitely bad. Three-letter, discretionary.)

What I do next is go to the paragraph that ends with that small word and try to adjust the tracking to see if it will pull that word up to the prior line.

In this case, changing the tracking to -5% for the paragraph that ended with "dog." was enough to bring that paragraph up one line. That eliminated my widow. But I decided to take it to -10% because it looks even better at -10%.

See?

Aleksa Baxter	A Dead Man and Doggie Delights

was bothering her. She'll usually stop if I just check out whatever it is and tell her she's been a good girl, but as I was walking across the yard I heard someone barking back at her.

That's right. Some jerk on the other side of the fence was barking at my dog. Seriously? I mean, what the…? Who does that?

I'd just spent five years living in Washington, DC and not once had someone barked at my dog. They'd stepped away from her like she had the plague, and there'd been an inordinate number of people who thought leaving chicken bones on the sidewalk was just fine and dandy, but none of them had barked at my dog.

And, because I was still in big city mode and not "love thy neighbor because you live in a town of a hundred where everyone knows everyone" mode, I stepped up on that little board along the bottom of the fence and told the guy off.

You know what he did? You know what that jerk did then?

He barked at me, too!

He lunged at me like he was going to attack me and barked. Three times. Woof, woof, woof.

I just stared at him like he was crazy. I mean, I'd moved to Baker Valley because it was supposed to be peaceful and nice and this is what I got on my first full day there? Some weird man barking at me? I didn't even know what to do at that point.

Unfortunately, while I was busy trying to figure out if werewolves might actually be real, which would at least explain the man's ridiculous behavior, my grandpa got involved.

🐾🐾🐾 6 🐾🐾🐾

With a shotgun.

There I was, hanging onto the fence, Fancy barking her head off at my feet, and my grandpa comes walking around the side of the house to confront the guy, shotgun in hand. At least I was pretty sure it was a shotgun, I'm not a gun person myself, but it had two long barrels that he pointed right at the guy. After cocking it or whatever it is you do with a shotgun to let someone know that when you pull that trigger it's gonna hurt.

"Son, you'd best get on your way." He planted his feet and pointed the gun right at the man, steady as steady could be.

I held my breath wondering if the man was stupid enough to bark at him, too. I figured it was a fifty-fifty chance and I really didn't know what my grandpa would do at that point, but I was pretty sure I didn't want to find out.

Fortunately, the guy just backed away, hands up. "Sorry, Mr. Carver. Didn't mean any offense. Just walking by."

"Well walk a little faster." My grandpa followed him with the gun, eyes flinty and jaw clenched tight. "And next time you leave my granddaughter alone or I'll put you in the ground where you belong, you hear me?"

"Grandpa," I hissed. "You can't say things like that."

This was exactly the type of thing I'd moved to Baker Valley to prevent. Well, okay, I'd had no idea before I moved that my grandpa was capable of pointing a gun at someone and threatening to put them in the ground where they belonged, but he had been slipping lately, and I'd been worried about him all

🐾🐾🐾 7 🐾🐾🐾

No more paragraph that ends with a short word and no more stranded final line of a paragraph.

Sometimes it isn't possible to fix it easily and then you just have to live with it. But often larger paragraphs or paragraphs with short words on the last line can be adjusted without the reader noticing the difference.

FIX JUSTIFIED PARAGRAPH ISSUES

If you chose to format your paragraphs as left justified you may run into a few other formatting issues you need to deal with. Basically, keep an eye out for paragraphs that stretched too much so that there's noticeable white space between words where there shouldn't be.

I can usually fix this by adjusting the tracking on that paragraph like I do for orphans and widows. Sometimes it's just a matter of pushing things together a little so that a big word moves up to the prior line.

Your other option that I mentioned briefly before is to apply hyphenation. Even if you don't want to use it for the whole book, you may want to apply it to a single paragraph, because if you have an especially long word that's causing the issue you may not be able to fix it with tracking.

Hyphenation is in the Paragraph studio. Just watch out if you do use hyphenation for a situation I believe is called pig bristles, where you have too much hyphenation in one paragraph. You can change the maximum consecutive hyphens setting to fix that.

CREATE MORE MASTER PAGES

For those of you getting ahead of me, you've probably realized we have an issue that we're going to run into soon. And that is what to do with a chapter that starts on the left-hand page like this one here:

We do not have a master page that will work in this situation. We have a Text and Chapter Start master page, but no master page for when the Chapter Start falls on the left-hand side.

You have a choice to make. Do you want your chapters to start wherever they fall, in which case this page will need a Chapter Start and Text master page? Or do you want all of your chapters to start on the right-hand page, in which case this page will need a No Text and Chapter Start master page?

In fiction, either one works. I've seen both in trade published books. In non-fiction and short story collections I have a strong preference for starting each chapter or story on the right-hand page.

In my novels I let my chapters start on whichever side of the page they happen to fall. With POD printing that can save you a few cents and usually my books are long enough I don't feel the need to stretch out their page count.

If you have an especially short title though, you may want to stretch it out a bit by starting all of your chapters on the right-hand side. Same is true of really short chapters. It starts to feel weird when all of the chapters are starting on the left-hand side of the page.

Either way, we don't have that master page so we need to go create a new one. Good news is, you can create new master pages at any point in time and it's not going to be a problem with your workflow. You won't have to go back and fix anything you've already done.

Let's create both, shall we?

NO TEXT AND CHAPTER START MASTER PAGE

The No Text and Chapter Start master page is incredibly easy to create. It looks like this:

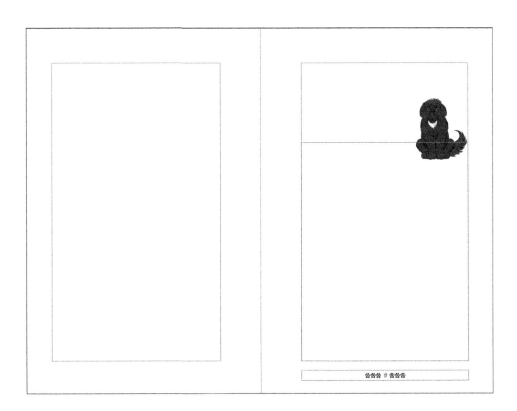

To create it, go to the Master Pages section of the Pages studio and copy the Text and Chapter Start master page. (Right-click, Duplicate, Rename).

Be sure to double-click on the renamed thumbnail before you start working.

Click on the Move Tool. Then click on every element (header, footer, text frame) on the left-hand page and delete it using the Delete key.

(You could also right-click and Cut each element or go to the Layers panel and right-click Cut or Delete or use the Delete key.)

Let's quickly apply that and our text styles to our Chapter 4 spread to see what it looks like:

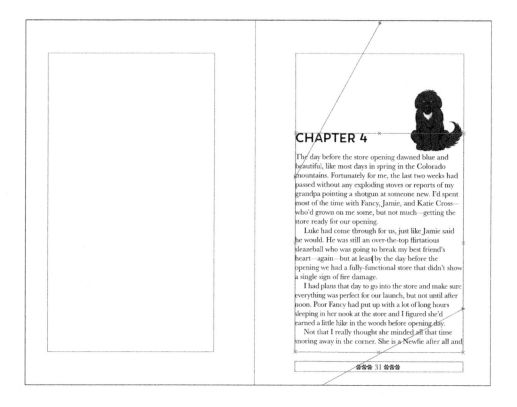

Perfect. Because we removed the text box from the left-hand side of the spread, the text instead flowed straight to the right-hand page. And the left-hand page is entirely blank. That's exactly what we wanted for a right-hand chapter start.

CHAPTER START AND TEXT MASTER PAGE

Next, let's create the Chapter Start and Text master page.

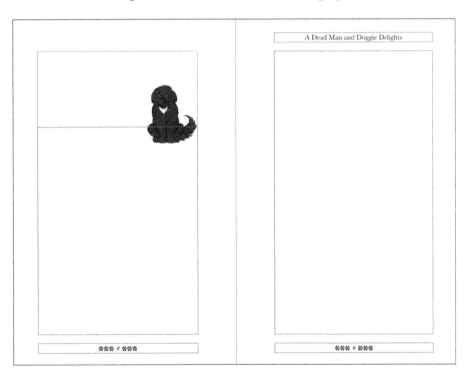

Go back to the Master Pages section. We have to change a lot on this one, but the Text and Chapter Start master page is a good place to start. So Duplicate, Rename, double-click.

First step is to change the size of the text frames. Click on the left-hand text frame and in the Transform studio change the height to the height you've been using for your chapter starts, so in my case 4.75. Click and drag the text frame so that it's aligned with the bottom of the text area.

(The reason to change the text frame heights rather than click and drag them to the other page is because of the text flow issues that would create that I mentioned above. If you do click and drag, you will then need to remove the text flow and redo it so that the text still flows from the left-hand page to the right-hand page.)

Second step is to change the height of the text frame on the right-hand page. That's a simple click on the top line and drag upward to the top of the text area.

Next, click and drag the image from the right-hand page to the left-hand page. Be sure before you move the image that you checked its Y value in the Transform studio so that you can position the image at the same height on the left-hand page as it had on the right-hand page. So you want the Y value the same and you want to align the image along the right-hand edge of the text frame on the left-hand page.

After that, it's just fixing the header. We want to delete the Author Name header on the left-hand page and add a Title header on the right-hand page. There are a couple ways to do this.

Sometimes you can go to another master page, copy an element and paste it into your new master page and it will paste in at the exact same spot on the second master page. So in this case, I could go to the Text and Text master page, click on the Title header, Ctrl + C, come back to this master page, Ctrl + V. And if I'm lucky it will paste in at the exact location I need it.

I can then just delete the Author header element.

If that doesn't work but it did paste in, you can then click and drag it to align with the Author header and the main text frame on the right-hand page before you delete the Author header.

Your other option would be to copy your Author header, drag the copy into place, then delete the original Author header, and change out the field for Author to Title.

Leaving the Author header up allows you to easily align the headers. If you don't want to copy you can get the Y coordinate from the Transform studio first and then position your new header that way.

Whatever way you prefer.

When you're done and apply the master page and your text styles, this is what you should see, a chapter that starts on the left-hand page and then the rest of the chapter flowing from there:

CHAPTER 4

The day before the store opening dawned blue and beautiful, like most days in spring in the Colorado mountains. Fortunately for me, the last two weeks had passed without any exploding stoves or reports of my grandpa pointing a shotgun at someone new. I'd spent most of the time with Fancy, Jamie, and Katie Cross—who'd grown on me some, but not much—getting the store ready for our opening.

Luke had come through for us, just like Jamie said he would. He was still an over-the-top flirtatious sleazeball who was going to break my best friend's heart—again—but at least by the day before the opening we had a fully-functional store that didn't show a single sign of fire damage.

I had plans that day to go into the store and make sure everything was perfect for our launch, but not until after noon. Poor Fancy had put up with a lot of long hours sleeping in her nook at the store and I figured she'd earned a little hike in the woods before opening day.

Not that I really thought she minded all that time snoring away in the corner. She is a Newfie after all and

🐾🐾 30 🐾🐾

A Dead Man and Doggie Delights

Newfs aren't exactly the most energetic of breeds. But I knew she also liked to get out and smell new things and we really hadn't had a chance to do so since our arrival.

So after I fed her breakfast at five-thirty in the morning—an unfortunate side effect of living those first crucial months of her life in an apartment with a neighbor who had a loud alarm and liked to get up at that time every morning of every day—we headed up the mountain behind my grandpa's house.

Most of the mountainside was covered not only with big evergreens and tightly-clustered aspens, but with juniper bushes and long grass that you wouldn't want to try to walk through. Fortunately for us, there was a nice little trail I'd seen Mr. Jackson tending the day of our arrival that was just wide enough for me and Fancy to walk side-by-side. Mr. Jackson had done a good job of cutting the branches, because not one slapped me in the face as we made our way towards the ridgeline about five hundred feet above my grandpa's house.

Fancy's a good girl so she didn't pull on her leash at all, just stopped to sniff and pee on things every few feet. She sometimes became a little too focused on one spot or another and I had to tell her to leave it and give a slight tug to move along, but usually I just let her do her thing. The walk was as much for her as it was for me, after all.

It was a gorgeous late spring morning. Birds were singing in the trees, bees were buzzing around on the early wildflowers scattered along the mountainside, and everything smelled fresh and clean and alive.

I was winded within five minutes because I wasn't used to hiking up mountainsides, and certainly not at

🐾🐾 31 🐾🐾

Now that you have everything you need, go through the whole document and apply your styles and master pages and any other adjustments.

FIX MISSING ITALICS OR BOLDED TEXT

Once you've gone through the whole document and applied your text styles, master pages, and fixed fiddly text issues, you will have a few more little things to fix.

If you applied a style like I did at the beginning using Ctrl + A and then Shift + 3, it is likely that you erased any italics or bolding that was applied to individual words within your paragraphs. I had you wait until now to fix those because if you needed to change the paragraph style on any of those paragraphs again (like for a first paragraph) you would've erased the formatting again and probably wouldn't have noticed a missed italics a second time.

A rare, but not impossible situation.

So now that you've made it through the whole document and your first paragraph styles are applied you can use Find to fix any missing italics or bold.

Go back to your source document and search for all entries with italics in them. (In Word, pull up the Find and Replace dialogue box and then type Ctrl + I in the Find What field to search for all italic entries.) You'll then have to manually go to your file in Affinity and search for those words to add the italics to each one using the Find and Replace studio. You can use Ctrl + I to apply italics to highlighted text.

As you do so, keep an eye out for if this shifts any paragraph. If so, I'd use Tracking to fix it.

If you have a lot of italics in your document or whole sentences or paragraphs, you may want to fix this earlier in your process because italics do take up a different amount of space than the plain text version. So maybe fix that first before you walk through the document. But keep in mind that if you have to apply a text style that you'll need to re-fix it. Another option might be to use a slightly different font size for the italics to make up for that difference.

(I just applied italics to a ten-line paragraph and it turned it into a nine-line paragraph. Tracking of 10% pushed it back to ten lines as did a font size of 13 pt instead of 12 pt.)

One more issue to note. Affinity has a flaw in its Find and Replace function. Find does not appear to work if there's an apostrophe in a word. So if you need to find the word "that's" in the phrase "That's what I was missing" to apply italics, you're going to need to search for "what I was missing" because searching for "that's" will return no result.

(This is one of those issues that could be fixed in a future update, so no harm in testing it each time they update to see if you still need a workaround.)

ASSIGN A PAGE ONE

We're almost done, but right now our first page of our main body of the novel is numbered 5.

CHAPTER 1

I hadn't been in the Baker Valley a day before the trouble began.

Fancy—that's my three-year-old Newfoundland, full name Miss Fancypants—and I were sitting out back in the yard at my grandpa's reading a book and minding our own business, enjoying the mid-spring day.

Well, I was reading. Fancy was curled up nearby, her head on her paws, watching the world go by. Not that there was much of a world to see. My grandpa's place is on the edge of town and backs up to a mountainside covered in tall evergreens and aspen trees, so all she really had to see was five hundred feet of trees followed by an incredibly blue sky without a cloud in sight.

Man, I love Colorado.

Anyway. There we were, minding our own business, not bothering a soul, when Fancy jumped up and raced to the fence, barking like a mad woman. And it wasn't her "Hey, is that a dog, can we play?" bark either. It was her, "There's a jerk too close to my home" bark.

I reluctantly set my book aside—I'd just gotten to the good part, too—and dragged myself over to see what

🐾🐾🐾 5 🐾🐾🐾

We don't want that. We want it to be numbered 1. Changing this doesn't affect the flow of the text through the rest of the document which is why you didn't need to fix it before this. And leaving it as is meant that your on-screen page number would continue to match the page number shown in the Pages section of the Pages studio which made it easier to find your page spreads on the left-hand side when you needed to apply a new master page.

(I actually usually fix it earlier because it annoys me, but realized as I was writing this book that leaving it as is until the end was the better approach.)

Okay.

The reason Chapter 1 currently starts on page 5 is because right now we don't have separate sections in our document and that first chapter starts on the fifth page in the overall document. Affinity doesn't know any better so it's just numbering from the beginning.

To fix this, go to the Pages section of the Pages studio and click on the page that has Chapter 1 on it. You only want that page, not the page spread. So click on the page itself, not the name of the page spread.

You'll know you've done this correctly when just that one page is surrounded by a blue box.

Right-click and choose Start New Section. This will bring up the Section Manager dialogue box.

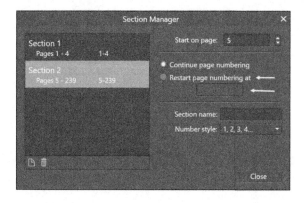

You can see on the left-hand side of the dialogue box that the document now has two sections and that Section 2 is selected and starts on page 5 of the overall document.

What we want to do here is to check the box for Restart Page Numbering At and then tell it to restart at 1. That's all we should have to do to fix this. Click Close.

And now the first page of the first chapter of the book should be numbered 1 even though it's the fifth page in the overall document.

(If you ever need to do this for a book that has front matter that uses a different numbering style you may also need to change the numbering style to 1, 2, 3, 4 but we didn't need that here.)

TIDY UP

When you reach the end of the pages that Affinity added for you, you'll either have blank page spreads at the end because you changed the paragraph formatting after Affinity flowed your text for you and that new formatting didn't require as many pages.

Or you'll have a red circle or red arrow along the edge of the last text frame on your last page (and actually you'll see it throughout the whole document) because as you added chapter starts and chapter header formatting that pushed the text down enough to require more pages than Affinity added for you.

For me, I have extra pages.

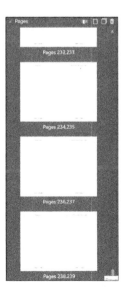

It's easy enough to delete all of these. Just click on the bottom one, scroll up to the next to last one that's blank, hold down the Shift key and click on it, too. That should select all page spreads between the two.

Now right-click and choose Delete X Pages from the dropdown menu where X is the number of pages in the selected range.

Done. The page spreads are gone.

(The reason we left that last one there is because you still need an About the Author page.)

If you don't have enough pages, then you just need to tell Affinity to reflow your document again. So go to that right-hand edge of that last text frame on that last page, click on the red circle to turn it into a red arrow, hold down the Shift key and click on the red arrow. Affinity should flow the remaining text to new page spreads for you. Finish formatting those new pages and then it's time for back matter.

(Remember that Affinity will use the format of that last page spread when it reflows text, so you may want to change that last page spread to a Text and Text master page first if it wasn't already.)

ADD BACK MATTER

After the main body of your document, you're going to need to add back matter.

For all of my books I at least have an About the Author page in the back. For my YA fantasy series I also included a glossary of names and a glossary of terms. For books two and three in that series I include a synopsis of the prior books.

For non-fiction I often include an index.

So what you do next is really going to depend on what you want for your back matter. In this book I am just going to walk you through how to add a simple About the Author page. At this point you should know how to create new master pages for whatever you need.

Just remember that for sections after the main body text you continue the page numbering from the main body. So if the main text ends on page 199, your Index will be numbered 201.

You have three potential scenarios that can happen at this point.

First, the last chapter ends on the right-hand side of the spread, so you put your back matter text on the right-hand side of the next page. That requires a No Text and Section Start master page.

Second, the last chapter ends on the left-hand side of the spread and you put your back matter on the right-hand side of that same spread. This requires a Text and Section Start master page.

Third, the last chapter ends on the left-hand side of the spread, but you leave that right-hand page blank and start the back matter on the right-hand side of the next page. This requires a Text and No Text master page as well as a No Text and Section Start master page.

We're going to build master pages for the last scenario which also covers the first scenario.

TEXT AND NO TEXT
MASTER PAGE

To create a Text and No Text master page, go to the Master Pages section of the Pages studio and copy and rename the Text and Text master page. Be sure to double-click on your Text and No Text master page before making changes.

Select the Move Tool. Click on each element (header, footer, text frame) on the right-hand side of the spread and delete them.

If needed, click on the master page thumbnail and drag it down to the end of the master pages listing.

NO TEXT AND SECTION START
MASTER PAGE

In the Master Pages section of the Pages studio, copy the No Text and Chapter Start master page, rename, double-click on the thumbnail to make sure you're editing the right one.

Click on the Move Tool. Delete the footer.

Click and drag the master page to the end of the master pages listing.

FINALIZE BACK MATTER

Once you have your back matter master pages created, assign them to the appropriate page spreads and add in any text you may need, such as the About the Author text. Apply your text styles to that text.

(I ended up tweaking the leading for the About the Author text because it went onto two lines and was too far apart for my liking. Because all of my chapter starts are one line I should be able to safely update the chapter header style to accommodate that, but I'd want to double-check the rest of the document after making that change to confirm.)

If you need more pages to add your back matter you can always right-click on the last page spread in the Pages section of the Pages studio and choose Add Pages.

Also, if Affinity is linking the about the author text frame to the main body text frames, which can sometimes happen but shouldn't, you can insert a break by clicking on the Artistic Text Tool, clicking into the text where you want the break, going to Text in the top menu, choosing Insert, Breaks, and then Frame Break or Page Break. Or you can unlink the frames by clicking on the blue arrow from the right-hand edge of the last frame in the main body of the document and clicking back into that same text frame. That should break the link.

Okay, so once you've done that, for the simple back matter we're doing here, you should have something similar to this.

Pages 186,187

Pages 188,189

A few more quick notes. Because the about the author section is going to be the same in each book we could have put that text into the master page spread instead.

If you do need to unlink the about the author text from the main body of the document, do it before you paste in the about the author text because otherwise it will be pulled back into the last frame of the main body of your document. (You'll see that little red circle or arrow indicating text that's hidden.)

And if you try to type * * * into Affinity it tries to turn that into a bulleted list. So if you're typing that within Affinity itself, leave out the spaces initially and then add them in after.

Okay. We're close. Just a few more steps to go.

PREFLIGHT

Your document at this point should be ready to export to PDF and review. But there's one more thing you can do and that's look at Preflight to check for any issues Affinity may have identified.

We put that studio on the top left at the end, so go click on it now.

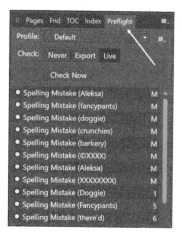

The top entries relate to your master pages and are indicated with an M in the right-hand column. The entries below that are for your actual document.

For fiction most of what you'll see are spelling errors. I spellcheck outside of Affinity (and you should have certainly done so before this point because a change now could change your layout) so I generally ignore the spelling issues it flags. I'll glance at them, just in case, but especially in fiction I use a lot of words that spellcheck doesn't like (as you can see).

But you see that it did flag XXXX as a spelling error. That's my personal reminder that I need to update my copyright information with my actual values before this file is ready.

There are other helpful issues that Preflight flags such as images that are out of proportion, tables of contents that need updated, and overflowing text frames. So always be sure to scan the list. Anything flagged in red (like an overflowing text frame), as opposed to yellow like the items in the screenshot above, will prompt Affinity to ask you if you want to review Preflight before you export.

I'm not going to cover it here, but you can also customize what Preflight flags. I've customized the DPI it uses to alert for images, for example.

Anyway. It's always worth a glance although I mostly use it on the non-fiction side. I mention it because if Affinity ever suggests you look at it before export, you really should.

EXPORT A PDF

When you think the book is ready to go it's time to create the PDF file. To do this, go to File and then Export. This will bring up the Export Settings dialogue box. Click on PDF.

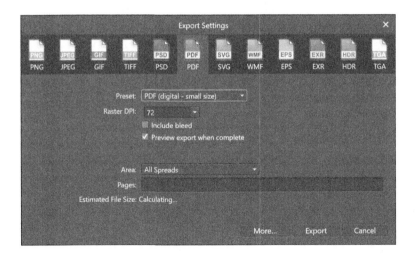

The single-most-important thing you need to do here is to change that dropdown for Area to All Pages instead of All Spreads.

(This is for people who are publishing via Amazon KDP or IngramSpark. I don't know if there are other printers out there where you don't need to do that, but for self-publishers it's absolutely crucial to make that change or you'll end up with a document that only prints half of your pages.)

And further to that point, when the PDF generates, make sure that the page count it shows is the same as the pages count in your Pages section of your Pages studio.

If you're doing a basic print book without a substantial number of images, you can use the Preset that's called PDF/X-1a:2003. That's the one IngramSpark says they like and it works just fine for Amazon as well. The Raster DPI should change to 300 when you do that.

For non-fiction I actually use a custom setting because I want to convert my images to grayscale before I submit to IngramSpark. Honestly, I have submitted files that had color images and they handled it just fine, but their recommendation is that you convert to grayscale first. For what we did here, I don't think it's something to worry about, but if you need that click on More down at the bottom to bring up a number of additional choices.

Once you've chosen your preset and changed the Area dropdown, click the box for Preview Export When Complete if it's not already checked. It should look like this now:

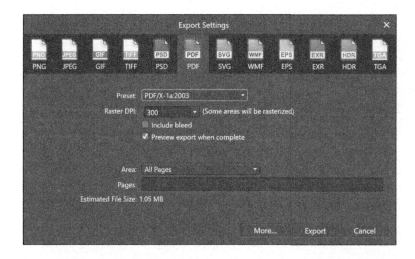

Click on Export.

Tell Affinity where to save the file and the name to use. Always verify the location you are saving your file.

(Do not assume that because the Affinity file you've been working on is saved to a specific folder that you will be exporting your finished file to that same location, because that's not how it works. Affinity exports to the last place you exported any Affinity file. I cannot count the number of times I've been caught out by that little fact.)

Click Save. Affinity will export the file and open it for you.

(I don't pay for a PDF program. My exported file opens in Adobe Acrobat Reader which I believe is free to use. When I was using Word and had images in my files I did run into an issue where the PDF export from Word wasn't high quality enough and I had to actually go to the paid Adobe site to convert my Word files to PDF to get the best quality for my images, but I haven't found that to be an issue working with Affinity Publisher.)

First things first, check the page count. It should match the page count in the Pages section of the Pages studio. If it doesn't, you probably need to re-export.

Next, scroll through the document page by page and make sure everything looks okay.

Are the headers and footers aligned? Do they include the full text they should? Are your paragraphs uniformly formatted? Did you catch all of the chapter starts and format them correctly and assign the proper master page?

If there are images in the file, do they look okay? (If at any point you move a linked image or rename it Affinity will show a blurred space where that image should be instead of the image itself.)

It's easier to check for extra pages or chapters or sections that start on the wrong side in Affinity itself using the Pages section of the Pages studio because of how it's laid out, but you can look for that here, too.

Make sure that any default fields, like Author Name, have been completed with the actual author name. And ISBN has been added in place of XXXX, etc. If you're changing out the image, make sure you did so and that it worked for all of the master pages that use that image. Make sure the Author and Title at the top of each page are the correct ones.

Check for italics and bolding in your main body text that might have been lost when you applied your paragraph styles.

Basically, does it look "right"?

If you do have to make any changes, then you'll need to export a new copy and review everything again.

REUSE AN OLD BOOK

As I mentioned before, when it comes time to publish a new book in a series I tend to just take my last book in that series, save a copy of the file under the new title, delete out the old content, and use that file to create the next book in the series.

If you're going to do that, it is very important that you really delete out the old text. To do so, go to the main body of your document and use Ctrl + A to select all of the text in the main body of the document and then delete it.

If you have even one linked text frame left, just deleting pages that have text showing in them DOES NOT get rid of the text itself. You have to select and delete the text before you delete the pages displaying that text.

After I delete the text I usually then delete all of the pages back to that initial set-up of seven pages we had when we flowed our text. So I leave the title page, also by, copyright and chapter start, and my first text and text spread. I then change all of my front matter for the new book and drop in the main body text of that new book and have Affinity flow it to new pages for me and then format.

I find that this is the easiest way to have all of the master pages and text styles I need. (You can copy in text styles and master pages from other Affinity files, but this was the easiest option I found. I also did try the Affinity template option at one point. It didn't work for me. I find this approach to be far easier.)

CONCLUSION

Alright. That's it. That's the basics of how to use Affinity Publisher to format a fiction title. Non-fiction, as I've alluded to a few times, can be much more complex. Especially if you try to add an index; I've found that part to be especially buggy and it's crashed my program more than once.

But for a basic fiction title, once you get those master pages set up the first time, it's incredibly easy to use. I expect that you'll want to tweak things a bit and that's fine. You should have the basic skills you need now to do that. See the Appendix for the quick and dirty rundown of the skills we covered here if you do need a refresher on anything. (I'm always forgetting exactly how to flow text.)

Also, if you don't feel like building your own master pages or things went horribly wrong as you followed this book, I do have some templates available on my Payhip store for purchase. They're basically a blank version of the file we just created with the text styles set up to be easily swapped out for a new font.

And if it turns out you learn better via video or want to see what we covered here in video, I have also done a video version of this book that can be found at ml-humphrey.teachable.com. You can use discount code HALFOFF to get fifty percent off.

As always with everything that is writing-related but not writing itself, remember that the bells and whistles are nice, but creating more books is the most important way to achieve success in this business. So don't let formatting your books distract you from creating more books. (Like I do far too often.)

Having said that, learning a skill like this can have tremendous benefits. It didn't work for all of my books, but being able to put together large print editions of my titles at no additional cost other than my time was a decision that has paid off nicely for me. Compare that to the time it takes to write a whole novel and sometimes the time spent better leveraging what you already have can be worth it.

Anyway.

If you have any questions, feel free to reach out at mlhumphreywriter@gmail.com. Good luck with it!

Affinity Publisher for Non-Fiction

AFFINITY PUBLISHER FOR
SELF-PUBLISHING - BOOK 4

M.L. HUMPHREY

CONTENTS

Introduction   153

Table of Contents   155

Use Chapter Names for Headers   177

Multiple Columns on a Page   185

Indexes   193

Merge Multiple Books Into One Title   207

Image Placement   233

Image Adjustments   249

Export as PDF   255

Conclusion   259

INTRODUCTION

Okay, first things first, if you haven't read *Affinity Publisher for Fiction Layouts*, you need to go read that first. Either that or you need to already be familiar with the basics of master pages, text styles, and how to flow text from one page to the next, as well as how to set up your workspace for working with print layouts.

This book assumes that you have a basic completed book that you're ready to add the bells and whistles to.

Second, the title of this book is a bit of a misnomer, because some of what we're going to cover here can also apply to fiction. For example, I have used a table of contents in my fantasy novels and if someone names their chapters they may well want to use those chapter names in their headers. But the rest is for non-fiction and it was a simpler title to use so there you have it.

So what are we going to cover in this book?

- How to create and format a table of contents

- How to use section or chapter names for the header instead of the book title

- How to have multiple columns of text on a page

- How to insert an index

- How to merge multiple book files into one

- How to insert images into the body of your text

It doesn't seem like a long list, but there's actually a lot of ground we're going to cover. And some of this stuff is the most finicky to work with. I have crashed the program more than once when trying to insert an index.

And I'm just going to warn you up front that these are also areas where I am personally the shakiest so I may not have the best answer on how to do these things. Of course, at this point I have formatted something like fifty non-fiction titles using Affinity Publisher, so when I say I'm shaky that's a personal standard not a general population standard.

Just know that there may be better ways to do the things I'm going to show you but I never got annoyed enough or curious enough to figure them out.

As an example, it took me until the last book I published to realize that there was an easier way to mark my index entries.

So if you're an expert at the stuff I listed above, this book may annoy you more than anything. But if you're stumbling through trying to make it all work and putting together little bits and pieces here or there like I tend to do when learning a new software, then this book should help accelerate your learning.

Okay then. Let's get started.

TABLE OF CONTENTS

Our first topic is going to be inserting and formatting a table of contents.

I'm first going to show you how to insert a basic, one-level table of contents. We'll then work our way through multi-level and customized table of contents and end with how to have multiple table of contents in one document.

A ONE-LEVEL TABLE OF CONTENTS

Here is an example of a one-level table of contents. This is pulled from *Affinity Publisher for Ad Creatives*:

CONTENTS

INTRODUCTION	1
BASIC DESIGN PRINCIPLES	5
AFFINITY WORKSPACE	13
COVER IMAGE FOR USE IN AN AMAZON A+ COMPARISON CHART	25
BANNER IMAGE CONTAINING MULTIPLE BOOK COVERS	41
BRIEF AD DISCUSSION	57
FACEBOOK SQUARE AD USING A BACKGROUND IMAGE	61
FACEBOOK SQUARE AD USING A SIDE IMAGE	81
BOOKBUB AD WITH IMAGE ADJUSTMENTS AND 99 CENT LABEL	89
EXPORT, SAVE, AND MORE	109
WRAP-UP	113

There is one single line for each chapter with no sub-sections showing in the table of contents.

Also, it's not something you can see here, but all of those chapter names were formatted using the same text style so there was no need to incorporate multiple text styles when generating the table of contents.

PRE-PREP

Before we can create a table of contents like this we need to do some prep work. Specifically, we need a master page formatted to be our table of contents page. The header you see there, "Contents", is not provided by Affinity, you need to provide that part of things yourself.

Here you can see the full table of contents page in my document:

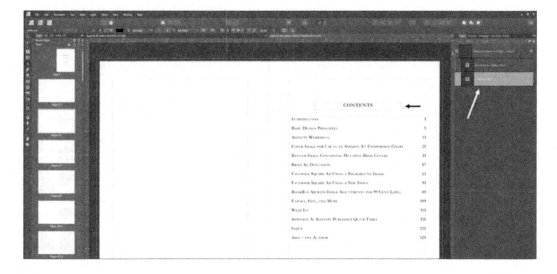

The master page for my table of contents has that text frame with "CONTENTS" in it and then another text frame below where I can drop in the actual table of contents.

Like so:

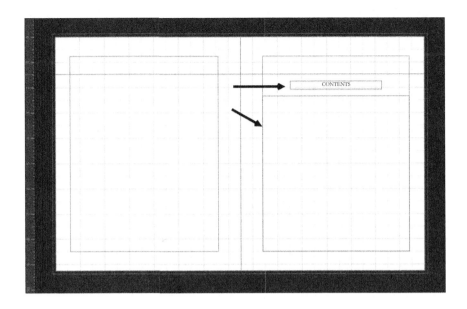

Which means your first step is to create the table of contents master page you want to use.

You can see that for mine I like to start the header a little lower on the page but not too far down, and that I leave a bit of space between that and where the actual table of contents text starts. Also, as mentioned, I use "CONTENTS" but you might want to use something else like "TABLE OF CONTENTS" or "CHAPTERS".

And you may want to have your copyright notice on the opposite page. I put my copyright notice opposite my Also By page so I leave the opposite page here blank.

Whatever you want, go format it now.

Once you have that set up, insert your table of contents master page in your document where you want your table of contents to be.

For me this is after my copyright and Also By page. I just glanced at a few of the books on my shelves and many of them put the table of contents after a dedications and acknowledgment page. Whatever works for you. I assume most would agree it should be before your main content starts and probably as close to that start point as you can get.

(Remember we're doing a singular table of contents right now for the whole book.)

That was prep step one.

Prep step two is to have a text style or styles that you've applied to the text you want to include in your table of contents. This style should not be applied to any other text in your document. Because Affinity won't be able to distinguish the difference between what you want to include or not include. So even if the formatting is identical between the text you want to include and other text in your document, you need to use separate styles for those two groups.

Since this is a one-level table of contents, that's generally going to be your chapter header text style.

In my case, it's showing as CSP-Chapter Title 1 because at some point I must've brought over text from an old KDP Word CreateSpace template.

I mention that there can be multiple text styles because sometimes that happens. Especially for novels I will use a different text style for my main chapters than I use for my back matter, like my About the Author section.

Affinity can work with multiple text styles, you just need to know going in that there are multiple styles involved and make sure that those styles are only applied to text you want to include.

But let's start simple with just one text style.

So at this point you should have a master page designed for your table of contents and you should have a specific text style assigned to your chapter headers. Now we're ready to create our table of contents.

INSERT A TABLE OF CONTENTS

Go to the page spread that's going to hold your table of contents and click into the location on the page where you want to insert it.

You now have two choices for how to do so.

Option one is to go to Text in the top set of menu options and then to Table of Contents in the dropdown menu and from there choose Insert Table of Contents. So Text->Table of Contents->Insert Table of Contents.

Option two is to go into the Table of Contents studio (which is one of the studios I have docked on the top left of my workspace if you're using my set-up from *Affinity Publisher for Fiction Layouts*) and click on the Insert option there which looks like three pages stacked with the middle one filled in:

The initial result you see may be "No Table of Contents Entries Found":

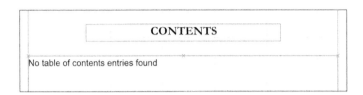

That is because you need to tell Affinity which style to use to identify the table of content entries. Its default is going to likely be Heading 1 and maybe Heading 2, so if those aren't the styles you're using for your chapter headers it won't pick them up.

You need to do this in the Table of Contents studio, but good news is that if you didn't already have it open, trying to insert a table of contents will have opened it for you. Here is the top portion of the studio:

You'll need to scroll down though to get to the section we want right now.

My docked version of the studio shows more of the available options, including the most important part right now, the Style Name section that includes check boxes for each style.

Note that in my screenshot none of the listed styles are currently selected. That's

because Affinity does not yet know which text style is the one I want to use for my table of contents. In a file that's completely new you may see that Heading 1 and Heading 2 are checked.

Go into this section, find the text style you applied to your headers, and click the checkbox on the left to select that text style.

If other styles that you didn't use are also checked, like Heading 1 and Heading 2, you can uncheck those or ignore them if they didn't bring in any entries to your table of contents.

When you check or uncheck the Style Names in the Table of Contents studio, Affinity will automatically adjust your table of contents for you. Like so:

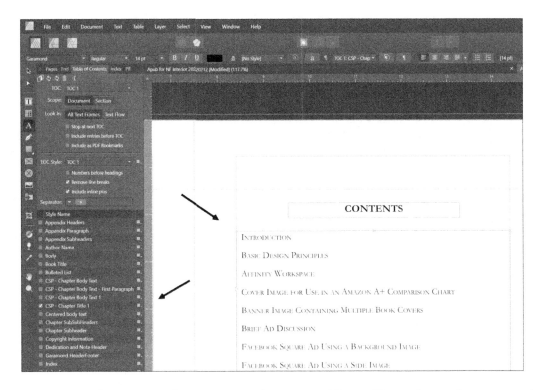

(Note that the formatting here is not what you will see. I'm using a document that had formatting already applied to the table of contents so that's what's showing for me. Below you'll see an example of the default formatting.)

INCLUDE MULTIPLE TEXT STYLES

If you want to incorporate text using more than one text style, simply check the boxes for all of the style names you want to use and those entries will be included in the table of contents.

In a file that's previously had a formatted table of contents using one of the text styles, the entries in the table of contents may not all look the same, but in a completely new file they should, like they do here:

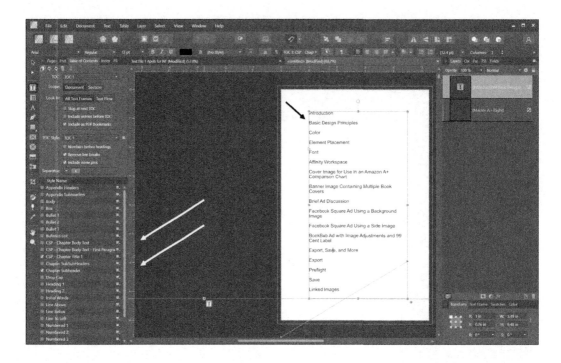

This is a brand new file that I pasted my text into to see what happens when there's no pre-existing formatting working behind the scenes.

I want you to note two things here.

First, that the formatting in the table of contents is identical for both text styles I've selected, CSP – Chapter Title 1 and Chapter Subheader.

And second, that the style assigned to both is TOC 1 which by default uses Arial, Regular, 12 pt.

This formatting differs from the one I was just showing you in my document. That is because I'm using a document where I've already adjusted my table of contents formatting to use Garamond and Small Caps.

Let's walk through how to make formatting changes like that in your document.

FORMATTING

PAGE NUMBERS

First off, I want page numbers for my entries.

To add page numbers, be sure you're clicked into the table of contents in your document so that the Table of Contents studio is active, and then go to the studio and find the style name you checked. Go to the end of the row with that style name listed where you can see four white lines with a dropdown arrow on the bottom right corner.

Click on that arrow and you should see a very small dropdown menu where you can click on the box next to "Include Page Number".

That should give you something like this where there are now page numbers at the end of each entry in the table of contents in your document:

Do this for each text style used in the table of contents. (Assuming you want page numbering to show for all of your entries.)

TEXT

We have page numbers now, but I don't like the default formatting Affinity uses.

The easiest way to change the formatting is to select some of the text in the table of contents in your document and change it there just like you would any other text.

So I'm going to highlight "Introduction" in my table of contents and then go to the Character studio and click the box for small caps and change the font to Garamond. The font selection and size are available up top, the all caps or small caps options are in the Typography section.

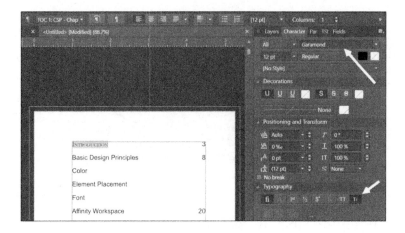

Small caps is the last option in the row. All caps is the one right before that.

I happen to like small caps. I would suggest using small caps or all caps in your table of contents, simply because they gloss over any issues around which words should be capitalized and which shouldn't in a title.

If you don't use one of those two formats, the capitalization of the text in your table of contents will match that of the entries the text is pulled from. Which means that if you ever see that you have a capitalization issue in your table of contents, you should ideally change it in the main body of the document, not the table of contents.

You can make any changes you want to the text in the table of contents once that text has been inserted, but the issue is that those changes will be overwritten if you ever update your table of contents again.

That's why it's a really bad idea to do extensive edits directly to the table of contents. It's very easy to forget you did so, see in preflight that Affinity thinks you should update your table of contents, click on the button to do so, and then lose all of your manual table of contents edits.

Much better to fix them in such a way that an automatic update doesn't change anything.

Speaking of…

UPDATE TOC TEXT STYLE

It was great that I could make those edits to the formatting of "Introduction", but I now want to apply those changes to all of my table of contents entries. And I also want to do so in such a way that I won't lose that formatting if I ever update the table.

To make that happen I need to update the text style used by Affinity for my table of contents entries.

While clicked onto that newly-formatted text entry, go to the dynamic menu up top, and click on the Update Paragraph Style option which is the little paragraph mark next to the current style name that has a swish mark:

You can see that the text style applied to this text right now was TOC 1:… which is a table of contents-specific text style. Updating that style to match the edits I just made will update all table of contents entries that are using that same style:

But note how in the screenshot above the second line updated to match the formatting I applied to Introduction, but the next three lines didn't.

That's because the content of those three lines was pulled from a different text style in my document and the table of contents treats them separately.

(Remember I had the Style Name boxes for both Chapter Title and Chapter Subheader checked in the Table of Contents studio.)

This is easy enough to fix. I can just format one of those entries the exact same way and then update that style as well.

Or if I wanted it to be slightly different, the fact that Affinity treats them as separate styles allows me to do that. So let's say I want a different font size for that one. I'm going to make it Garamond, 10 pt, and put it in all caps instead of small caps.

Here we go:

INDENT

But now I have an issue. It's not very easy to distinguish the subheader entries from the rest. The all caps and font size difference just don't make it stand out much.

What I really want is for those subheader entries to be indented, but when I try that indent level option in the Table of Contents studio, it doesn't do anything. What I can do, though, is select a line of that text in the table of contents, go to the Paragraph studio, and set a left indent of .2.

Update my text style and this is what I get:

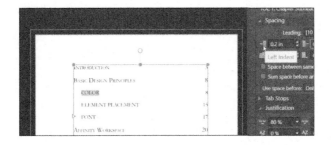

That's better. It sets those sub-entries apart nicely.

I showed you that because basically any formatting you can do on normal text you can also do on your table of contents entries. Just remember to update the style to keep those changes so they aren't lost if you update your table of contents later.

For me that would probably be good enough and I'd be done, but there are a few more formatting items I want to mention.

SPACE AND SEPARATORS BETWEEN TEXT AND PAGE NUMBERS

The Separator option in the Table of Contents studio is where you can tell Affinity how to separate your text from your page numbers.

Here, for example, I've removed the Tab separator and just used an Em Dash to separate the text from the numbers.

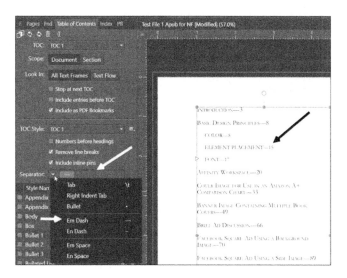

Not my preference, but an option. As is any combination of the elements in that list.

On this particular table of contents some of the page numbers ended up on the left-hand side because of the text taking up too much of the line.

To fix that you could manually adjust it by highlighting the page number and then choosing right-align to format it.

But that is a manual adjustment that will be overridden each time you refresh the table of contents unless you update the page number text style.

I poked around a bit for a solution on this one and think that I stumbled across something that works. It was to have an Em Space followed by a Tab in the Separator section. That seemed to work for the table of contents I have here, but no promises it will work for any other set-up:

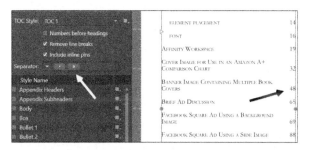

You can also click into that field next to Separator and manually type in something like a space or a period. Like here where I added a few periods in a row:
Again not my favorite. And I will note here that after I typed each period it kicked

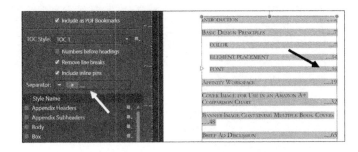

me out of the field, so I had to type a period, click back into the field, type the next one, etc. So not only not great looking, but not easy to do.

If you want to add a dotted line all the way across, though, there's an easier way to do it.

Click on the text for one of your table of contents entries, go to the Text Styles studio, right-click on the table of contents entry option for that style or for all entries (in this example, TOC 1: Entry), and choose Edit from the dropdown menu.

That is going to bring up the Edit Text Style dialogue box. On the left-hand side under Paragraph there is a listing for Tab Stops. Click on it.

There should be a tab stop entry already showing under Paragraph Tab Stops.

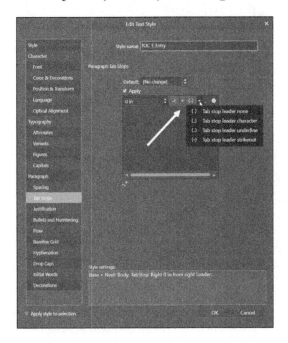

Click on the second dropdown arrow, the one next to the set of parens, and choose the option for tab stop leader character which has a period within the parens.

You will get a result that looks like this where there are periods between the end of the table of contents entry and the page number:

If there wasn't a tab stop entry already you can click on the + sign below the box

to add one.

If you choose the TOC 1: Entry text style that will edit all of your table of content styles at once. If you just want the dotted line for one of your styles then make your edits to that particular text style instead.

That was how to add a dotted line. That dropdown also gives you the option to add a solid line at either underline height or strikeout height.

The Tab Stops section of the Edit Text Style dialogue box is also where you can adjust the amount your page numbers are indented from the right side of the text frame. You do this by increasing the value for the position setting from its default of zero.

You can also have multiple tab stops if you need them.

PAGE NUMBER FORMATTING

Page numbers do have their own text style. By default it will mirror the text style for the corresponding entry, but you can edit it directly if that's ever needed, like above with the right-alignment setting I mentioned to ensure your page numbers are always on the right-hand side.

Okay, so that was formatting.

UPDATE YOUR TABLE OF CONTENTS

It is very likely that after you initially insert your table of contents you will need to update it at some point. Maybe you add or delete some text, or change a chapter name to fix a typo, or add some back matter. Whatever the reason, you will very likely need to update your table of contents before you are through.

Your first option is to go to the Table of Contents studio and click on the update option at the top:

There are actually two update options to choose from. When you only have one table of contents in your document it doesn't really matter which one of them you use, they both do the same thing. (Once you have multiple table of contents the update one should apply to the currently listed table of contents, the other will update all table of contents in the document. We'll cover this in a bit.)

Your second option is to go to Text-> Table of Contents and choose to update the table of contents from there.

Your final option is in the Preflight studio. There will often be a message at the top that "One or more tables of contents entries need updating." Simply click on "Fix" to update the table of contents that way.

Whichever method you use, be sure to visually review your table of contents again afterward to make sure you didn't have any manual change to the table of contents that has now been erased.

Okay, so that was the basics of a single table of contents with one or more levels of entries. Now let's talk about multiple table of contents. This is trickier and we'll cover it again when we talk about merging multiple books into one.

MULTIPLE TABLE OF CONTENTS

I use multiple table of contents when I am publishing a collection of non-fiction titles. I generally don't need this for omnibus editions of my fiction titles, but again, if someone uses chapter titles and wants to list those out at the beginning of each novel then they might need multiple tables of contents to do so.

But for me, for example, my *Excel Essentials 2019* series has three books in it that I've published separately that are part of the published collection. That collection has one overarching table of contents where I list the name of each individual title and its starting page number as well as the back matter and then at the beginning of each individual title I have the book-specific table of contents.

So here's the overarching table of contents:

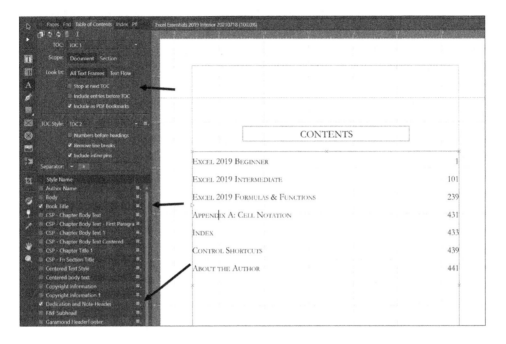

The key things to note here are that I used two text styles for this main table of contents. They don't look any different in the actual table of contents, but definitely are in the book itself since the book titles are pulled from a title page and the back matter entries are simple chapter headings.

Since I wanted my back matter, like the about the author section and my control shortcuts, to be in this first table of contents, I assigned a different text style from my chapter headers to those entries in the document.

So that's step one in a situation like this. Figure out what you want to include in that main table of contents and then make sure that all of the text that you want to include has a text style assigned to it that is not assigned to any other text in your document.

You can have multiple text styles that feed into the main table of contents, but make sure those text styles are not assigned to any other text in the document.

The second thing I want to note here is that for the main, overarching table of contents you want to NOT check that "Stop at next TOC" box. Because the entries in this table of contents are likely going to be drawing from the entire book.

And you can see here that that's true. My first table of contents entry is coming from page 1 but my last one is coming from page 441 and there are three books' worth of content in between the two.

Now let's look at the table of contents for the first book in this collection, *Excel 2019 Beginner*.

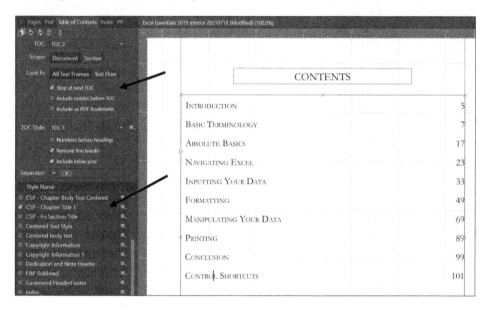

The text style used for this table of contents is different from the text styles used for the main table of contents. This text style can be used throughout the main body of the document. It's used for all of my chapters in all three books.

It works that way because of the second setting I want you to notice here. For the secondary tables of contents, I do check the "Stop at next TOC" box. That allows Affinity to pull all of my chapter headers from this title, but to stop pulling entries at the table of contents for the next title in the collection.

Here is that second book-specific table of contents:

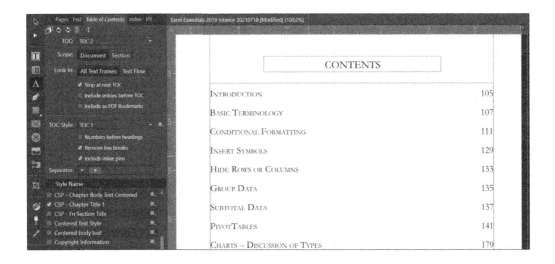

CONTENTS

INTRODUCTION	105
BASIC TERMINOLOGY	107
CONDITIONAL FORMATTING	111
INSERT SYMBOLS	129
HIDE ROWS OR COLUMNS	133
GROUP DATA	135
SUBTOTAL DATA	137
PIVOTTABLES	141
CHARTS – DISCUSSION OF TYPES	179

Note how it begins on page 105? And the prior table of contents stopped on page 101?

That's because we told Affinity to stop at the next table of contents. The style name used for this table of contents is the same as the style name used for the first title table of contents.

Note that the box for "include entries before TOC" is also not checked. That's the case by default and you should never have to even think about it, but I mention here just in case. You want the table of contents contained to entries for this title only.

So that's it. The key to having multiple table of contents is (1) using different text styles for the overarching table of contents versus the other table of contents, (2) letting the overarching table of contents pull entries from the entire book, and (3) limiting the additional table of contents to only their section by clicking on "Stop at next TOC" and not including entries from before each TOC.

Sometimes this will require making adjustments. Usually I have to change the text style for my back matter to a new text style, for example. But it's usually not too much work. You'll see this in action when we reach the chapter on merging existing books into one.

Also, you can have different formatting for each Style Name in each table of contents in your document. These happen to be formatted the same way, but Affinity assigns a different text style for each Style Name in each table of contents, so each one is fully customizable by itself.

MULTI-PAGE TABLE OF CONTENTS

One final issue to mention. Sometimes you'll have a table of contents that flows across multiple pages so you'll want to create a master page or master pages for that scenario.

I have two additional master pages, one for two pages of table of contents entries and one for a single page of table of contents entries and a chapter start page.

There should be text flow between your table of contents pages but not between the table of contents and your first chapter. I also include a "CONTENTS (CONT.)" header as well as page numbering on all subsequent table of contents pages.

Once you have those master pages, simply insert the one(s) you need after the initial table of contents master page and then flow your text from that first page to the others.

Here for example is the end of a five-page table of contents:

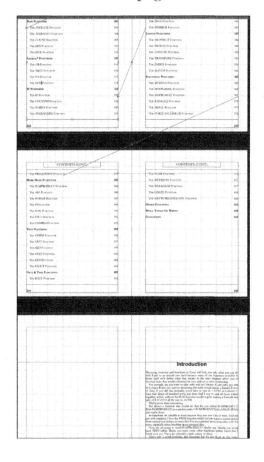

You can see the blue lines that connect the table of contents pages, but note how the final page of the table of contents does not flow forward from there. I do not connect my table of contents to the main body of my book.

You can also see that I let the subsequent pages in my table of contents take up the whole page when I set up my master pages.

Also note that for a table of contents that's at the beginning of the book, page numbering should be in lower-case Roman numerals (ii, iii, iv, etc.). But for a table of contents later in a book, like this one, the page numbering just continues from the prior page. So here the pages are 242, 243, etc.

Basically, you have one set of numbers for your intro material and another for the rest of the book. We'll cover this more in the merging existing titles chapter.

* * *

For now that should be the end of our discussion of table of contents. Let's move on to an easier subject, using chapter names for your headers instead of your book title.

USE CHAPTER NAMES FOR HEADERS

I now want to talk about how to have different headers for each of your chapters or sections rather than just using the book title throughout the whole book.

(And I'm going to say headers throughout this section, but if for some reason you put the book title or chapter names in your footers or on the side of the page instead, it works the same way there. Basically anywhere you'd have Affinity auto-populate your book title you can instead have it auto-populate using your section names.)

Like here where you can see that my chapter name is Introduction and the odd-numbered pages in that section also have Introduction for the header. (As opposed to the book name which is how we set up the fiction book we did in *Affinity Publisher for Fiction Layouts*.)

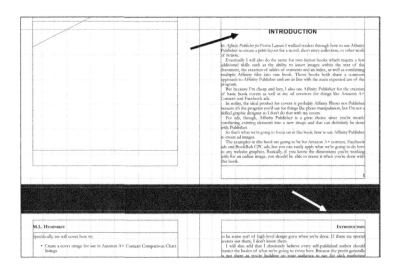

The first step is to modify any of your impacted master pages.

For me that's just my Text and Text master page. That's the only master page I have for non-fiction that has book title or section title text in the header since I start all of my chapters on the right-hand side of the page for non-fiction.

If you were doing this for fiction chapter names, which you could, and you were letting your chapter starts fall where they may, then you'd probably have a chapter start and text master page that also needed edited.

And depending on how you've formatted your back matter master pages, one of those may also require an edit. (You'll catch it in the PDF review if you miss it now, but this is why you need to scan through the entire final file when you're done because one page can look fine and then another that uses a different master page will not.)

Okay. Chances are, if you followed *Affinity Publisher for Fiction Layouts*, you have a text and text master page that looks something like this where the actual title of your book shows in the right-hand header of the master page:

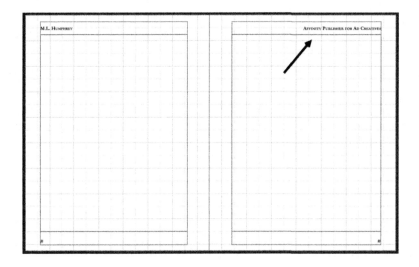

That's actually using a field to populate the text, but because the title is the same throughout the document Affinity just shows the title itself rather than the field marker for book title in the master page. (I would personally prefer they didn't do it that way, but it is what it is.)

To use the chapter names instead, what we actually need to do is tell Affinity to use section names. I refer to this as the chapter names because that's how I break up my sections, but technically sections do not have to be tied to chapters. So you could have a section that encompasses ten chapters and use that name in your headers or you could split a chapter into three sections and use those names instead.

But for the sake of simplicity, I'm going to talk about chapters.

First step, go to the Master Pages section of the Pages studio and double-click on the master page you want to edit to open it in your workspace.

Next, click on the Artistic Text Tool (the capital A on the left-hand side) and then click into the text frame where you have your book title and highlight and delete it.

If you didn't have text to delete, just click into that text frame. Now go to the menu up top, and under Text->Insert->Fields, choose Section Name.

Your master page should look like this now with the <Section Name> in place of your book title. The <> marks indicate that this is a field that will be populated with a value in the actual document:

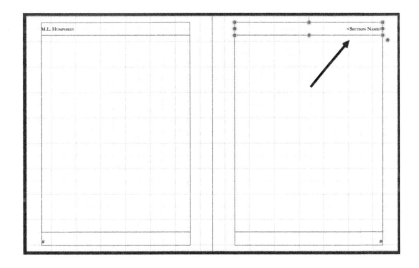

Do this for every master page where you need to change out the book title for the section name or want to add a section name.

That was step one. Affinity won't bring in section names to your final document unless you've specified a location for it to use. But chances are, you really don't have any section names for it to bring in at this point, because you didn't need sections for each chapter before this.

If you were just using the book title then the only sections you probably used were for your front matter where the page numbering needed to be different. For example, here are the sections I have in my large print version for my first cozy mystery:

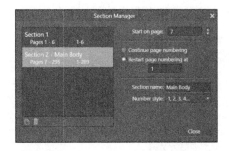

There are only two of them and only one has an assigned name.

Which means for a book that uses chapter/section names instead of book title in the header, we've got some work to do.

Here, for example, is the Section Manager for *Affinity Publisher for Fiction Layouts*:

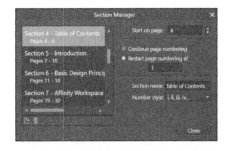

It has seventeen sections, because in order to have my headers show Introduction, Basic Design Principles, Affinity Workspace, etc. I had to go into Affinity and create sections for each of my chapters.

One thing to keep in mind when working with sections is that every single page in your document will be part of a section. If a document is 100 pages long and you start a section on page 10 and don't add any other sections then pages 1-9 will be one section and pages 10 through 100 will be another.

This means if I only want pages 10 to 20 to be part of a section, then I need to go to page 21 and assign a new section there even if I'm not going to see that section name anywhere in my final document.

For the most part that's not going to be an issue for you. You'll naturally have all of those breaks because we're going to assign a section for each chapter start. But at the very end of the book you may want to watch out for this because you could have "Conclusion" carry over into your back matter. Also, if you have any section divider pages throughout the document you may want those to have their own section.

A lot of it will come down to which master pages you're using and whether they're set to show a book title or section name. You can have messed up sections as long as the master pages aren't set to show that fact in the final product.

Still. Keep it in mind when assigning sections and when troubleshooting errant header or page numbering that you didn't want. There's nothing wrong with having more sections than you need to ensure that you keep things clean.

Okay. Let's go through now and do step two which is assigning new sections to each of our chapters and providing our section names.

Go to your first chapter start in the Pages section of the Pages studio, right-click on that singular page (not the two-page spread), and choose Start New Section from the dropdown menu.

This will bring up the Section Manager dialogue box:

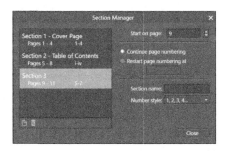

Our chapter is Section 3, because we already had sections for the cover page and the table of contents.

We've already told Affinity where to start this section, on the first page of the chapter. But now we need to tell Affinity the Section Name we want to use in the header. Click on the space next to Section Name and it will turn into a white input field.

You want to put in that field the actual text you'd like to see in the header.

Usually I can just copy and paste the chapter name into that field and I'm fine. But watch out for situations where you have a chapter name that is too long for the header text frame. In that case you'll want to choose a header that's a little more reasonable.

Like here where you can see from the table of contents that my actual chapter name is "Cover Image for Use in an Amazon A+ Comparison Chart" but I changed the header to just "Amazon A+ Comparison Chart":

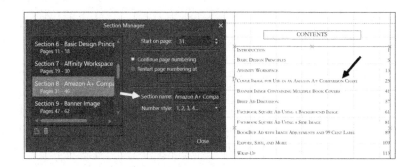

I should note here that when I run into this issue it is often a sign to me that I should actually modify the chapter name to something simpler.

In early drafts I'm a little too fond of titling chapters with things like "Learn to Create a ..." or "Insert a..." when I could just simply list the chapter name as whatever they are going to insert or learn to create.

But I still do end up with overly-lengthy chapter names even when I make those changes, so I still have to keep an eye on the actual final product to make sure my text fully shows up in my header.

(And I will note this is one of the reasons I moved away from using Vellum for print because I once bought a non-fiction book that had been created in Vellum and used long chapter names and Vellum had just cut off the end of the chapter name in the header and put ... at the end. It was not a good look. And not something I could figure out how to control in that program.)

Back to our chapter sections. You need a new section for every time you want to change what the header text will display. And you need to put in that Section Name field whatever text it is you want displayed for that section.

For the first chapter of your book, also make sure you restart your page numbering at 1 and change back to Arabic numerals (1, 2, 3...) from Roman in the Number Style dropdown if that isn't the case already.

For every chapter or section after that point the numbering should continue the page numbering and use Arabic numerals. I don't think you'll have to change this, I think it will be automatic, but check to be sure as you're creating your sections.

(And for section dividers and things like that where you don't want a page number showing on the page, that's handled in your master page layout not here. Simply don't include a place for page number on the master page that you use for those.)

You shouldn't have to specify the ending page for your sections, because those will be set by the starting page for the next section. So as long as you add new sections throughout, that should be taken care of automatically.

As you add each section, the title you provided for that section should appear wherever you have your section name field on your master page. This does mean that for some shorter chapters you'll never actually see the section name in your document. Still create that section, though. Because if you add a little bit of text to a chapter and it pushes it to three pages long, suddenly you're going to need to have assigned that section name.

If you later notice an issue with one of your section titles or the page numbering used in a section, you can simply right-click on any page in the Pages section of the Pages studio and choose Edit Section to re-open the Section Manager. The Section Manager covers the entire document, so once it's open you can edit any section you want.

Simply click on the section you need to edit and change whatever you need to change.

The two changes we haven't discussed yet are deleting a section, which you can do by clicking on that section name and then using the trash can below the listing of sections. Here:

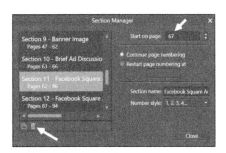

And changing the "start on page" value for the section which you can do at the top of the dialogue box. See the arrow above. That will shift the end of the prior section as well. Remember, every page has to be assigned to a section. Also, each page can only be assigned to one section.

You can also add a new section directly in the Section Manager dialogue box, but I prefer to do so from within the Pages studio. The Section Manager dialogue box uses the page number for each page based upon the entire document length. So Chapter 5 may be on page 47 according to the Section Manager but I see it in my formatted document as page 36.

Rather than try to do that mental gymnastics, I'd rather just to go to the page for Chapter 5, right-click, and insert the section that way.

But if you're more confident about those things than me, you can use the little page icon next to the trash can below the listing of the current sections in the Section Manager to insert your new section. And then you'd need to provide the start on page as well as any edits to the number style, whether the page numbering continues or not, and the section name.

Okay, so that's it.

To use section/chapter names in your headers you first modify your master pages and then assign sections and section names throughout your document.

MULTIPLE COLUMNS ON A PAGE

Those first two items were ones that could apply to fiction books as well as non-fiction. There's one more topic like that, merging multiple books into one title, so if you're dealing with fiction you may want to skip ahead to that chapter.

Right now we're going to turn our attention to a few tricks that apply more to non-fiction books, specifically having more than one column on the page and indexes.

We'll cover multiple columns first.

I use this one for my Index section in each book because most of my index entries are pretty short and I don't need to take up a full line for each of them. I'd end up with a ten-page index that had a lot of white space on the page.

Here's an example of an index page from one of my books:

INDEX	
A	Export 110
Affinity Help 107–108	PDF 64, 103–105, 110
Author Name 109	I
Field Edit 109	Image 110
Insert 109	Adjustments 97–101, 110
B	Border 95
Book Title 109	Center 110
Field Edit 109	DPI 83, 86, 91, 110
Insert 109	Float 93–94, 110

This is the index page with text frames showing. And it is the top of the first page of the index.

You can see that the entries start in the left-hand column and go downward, there's then a space between that column and the second column, and then the entries continue in that second column on the right-hand side.

In this case, both of the columns are the same width.

I set this up on the master page for my index, so it's already built in when I use it.

It's very easy to do. Go to the master page where you want multiple columns, and if you don't already have one there, insert a text frame onto your page. If you already have a text frame, make sure it's selected.

Next, find the Columns option at the far right side of the dynamic menu up top and change the value from 1 to 2 or whichever number of columns you want to use:

Affinity will take that text frame and create that number of columns for you in that space using the default settings, which are what you saw in my screenshot above. You can customize those settings, however.

Next to the Columns option is an option for specifying the width of the gap between your columns.

In my screenshot above that setting is currently hidden and I need to either click on the double-arrow at the very end of the dynamic menu to see more options or widen my Affinity window to make it visible.

Here I went ahead and widened the window but you can still see that there are more options behind that double-arrow at the end:

The gutter width setting is right next to the number of columns setting. You can change that setting to zero if you want no gap between the two columns (not something I'd recommend unless you have other settings on your text to maintain some distance) or you can increase the gap if you don't think it's big enough as is.

If you resize your text frame by clicking and dragging from the right-hand side, that will also resize all of your columns. The gutter will not change when you do this, though.

If you want to get really detailed or have different-sized columns, you can open the Text Frame studio and go to the Columns section there:

As an example, I'm going to create a layout with two equally-sized columns and

one smaller third column.

As I change the first column that automatically changes the other columns to keep the same total width as I started with because the "Preserve Width" box is checked. If I didn't want that, I could uncheck that box and then the width of the text frame would just be the total of my column widths and gutters.

Below is an example of two larger columns and one smaller.

It didn't let me have uneven gutters so those had to stay the same but you can see that my first and second columns are 2.327 inches and then my last one is .946 inches with a .2 inch gutter between the columns:

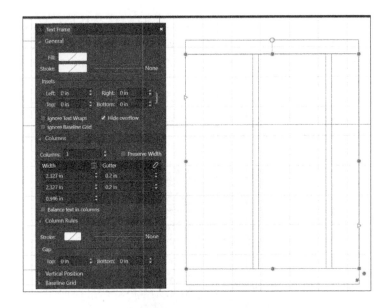

It's also possible to have a visible line dividing your columns. You can create one by using the Stroke setting in the Column Rules section of the Text Frame studio.

Click on the line with the red mark through it next to the Stroke color box and then change the Width value to a non-zero value.

Here I've changed it to 3.8 pt and you can see that there are now dark black

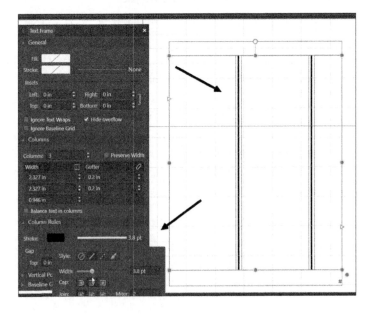

lines in the gutters between my columns. I used the Width slider until I could visibly see lines between the columns but you could as easily enter a specific value.

In that same Stroke dialogue box, if you go to Start and End you can change the settings there so that the line has a shape at the end.

And if you don't want the line to extend from top to bottom but to just fill part of the space, you can set the Top and Bottom values under Gap in the Column Rules section to create a shorter line.

Here I've changed the lines to have an arrow at each end and to have a 1.25 inch gap at the top and bottom:

There's a lot you can play with in this section, but honestly I just normally keep it

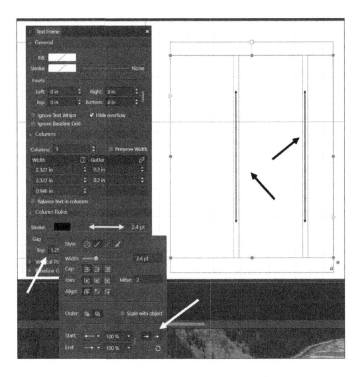

simple. No lines, no arrows, no gaps. Just two columns equally spaced.

There is one final setting that may come in handy, though, and that's the checkbox to "Balance Text in Columns" which is in the Columns section of the Text Frame studio just below the column measurements we covered above.

This comes into play when you don't have enough text to fill the entire page. You can check this box and Affinity will evenly spread what text there is across however many columns you have.

Here's an example with two columns.

This first example is balanced. You can see that the text in both columns ends at about the same point on the page:

This second example is not balanced and just lets the text fall where it may:

weights for that font. Or select text and go to Character studio font weight dropdown at top.

TEXT FRAME

ALIGN OR POSITION

Frame Text Tool or Move Tool. Left-click on text frame and hold as you drag. Look for red and green alignment lines to center or align to other elements in workspace. (Turn on Snapping if there are no red or green lines.) Use Alignment dropdown in top menu to align to workspace, not the dynamic menu bar that applies to actual text.

INSERT

Frame Text Tool on left-hand side.

Click and drag in workspace.

RESIZE

Click on text frame layer. Left-click and drag on one of the blue circles around the perimeter of the text. Click and drag at an angle from the corner to keep scaling proportionate.

UNDO

Ctrl + Z. Or you can open the History studio and rewind using the slider or by clicking back onto a prior step.

I should also note here that when I was trying to check and uncheck that

weights for that font. Or select text and go to Character studio font weight dropdown at top.

TEXT FRAME

ALIGN OR POSITION

Frame Text Tool or Move Tool. Left-click on text frame and hold as you drag. Look for red and green alignment lines to center or align to other elements in workspace. (Turn on Snapping if there are no red or green lines.) Use Alignment dropdown in top menu to align to workspace, not the dynamic menu bar that applies to actual text.

INSERT

Frame Text Tool on left-hand side. Click and drag in workspace.

RESIZE

Click on text frame layer. Left-click and drag on one of the blue circles around the perimeter of the text. Click and drag at an angle from the corner to keep scaling proportionate.

balance box sometimes it didn't seem to take. So always be sure you've clicked on your text frame before you make the adjustment, because it seems a little finicky. (Or it could be me.)

Also, when I had the three columns set up I wasn't able to get Affinity to not flow text to that final column. So if what you actually want is a layout that has, for example, a third column for pull-out quotes or something like that, then columns are not the way to go.

In that instance what you'd want are two linked text frames for your main body text and then a third text frame that is standalone for any pullout text.

Okay, so that was columns. Now let's talk talk about how to create an index in your document.

INDEXES

Now on to indexes, which should probably be called indices instead, but I don't like indices as much as I like indexes. And this is my book so I get to do what I want. (And it turns out the dictionary thinks I'm okay doing it that way. They're both acceptable.)

Inserting an index into an Affinity document is where I have encountered the most crashes and had the most challenges. This could very much be a me issue not a them issue. But it's a fact that I used to crash my files on a regular basis when inserting an index.

Fortunately, Affinity's recovery settings are excellent and I rarely lost anything. Also, I finally figured out a workaround that seems to solve my personal issue, which was that I would accidentally insert an index into my document in the wrong location when I was actually trying to mark a new entry for the index, and when I would then try to undo that using Ctrl + Z it would crash the program instead.

I rarely lost anything other than that index I didn't want there anyway, but I had to train myself to never ever use Undo if I accidentally inserted an index where I didn't want it.

The more long-term solution to this issue was to flag one entry for my index, go to where I did want my index inserted, and insert the index immediately. That prevented me from accidentally inserting an index into the document instead of marking an entry later, because Affinity only allows one index and I already had one.

When I was done marking all my index entries I then just had to update that index so it reflected all of my entries. (Which sometimes required deleting the existing entries before it would work, but since it was one entry that wasn't too hard to do.)

I'll also note here that you may not even have to update your index at the end. On the last index I inserted into a document, it automatically updated for me as I tagged new entries.

Hopefully crashing Affinity when using an index will not be an issue for you, but I wanted to cover it up front so you understand why I'm approaching this in what may seem like a weird way.

This is also definitely one of the areas that they may improve over time or where I may not be doing things in the optimal way, so if you find a better way to do it, you're probably right.

But I have formatted twenty-plus books with an index in the last year and more before that, so the information in this chapter definitely works.

Okay, then, let's do this. Here is the first page of an index:

INDEX

3D Covers 42	DPI 27
A	Dynamic Toolbar 15
A+ Content Manager 26	**E**
B	Elements 115
Background Color 43, 115	Alignment 51
C	Align Horizontally 51
Color 115	Align Center 52, 67
Apply Specific 73–74, 84, 90, 92, 115	Space Vertically 51–52
Bright Yellow 74	Align Vertically 51
Change 43–44, 66–67, 115	Align Middle 51–52
Eyedropper 90–91, 93	Center 49, 86, 93, 115
Opacity 21	Copy And Move Simultaneously 47
Color Chooser 22	Distribute Evenly 49–51, 115
D	Group and Move 48, 116
Design Principles 5	Group and Resize 48, 116
Color 5–8	Height 45, 99, 111
Element Placement 9–10, 99	Move 72
Font 10–11	Resize 99

125

Note that entries are listed alphabetically under a single letter of the alphabet with indents for each topic and sub-topic.

If there are two or more pages that you flag consecutively for the same index category, Affinity will automatically show those as pages X-Y as you can see for Color, Apply Specific or Color, Change.

(I swear it used to only do that for three or more pages and I'd have to manually adjust when there were just two pages, but that seems to not be the case in this current version of Affinity I'm working in. So double-check this just in case.)

As we discussed last chapter, I format the master page for my index section in two columns. I find that works well for the labels I give my entries and keeps the index from taking up too much of my document.

Also, the header there, "Index", was added by me on the master page. Your index will insert into your document without any sort of header.

Indexes are managed via the Index studio:

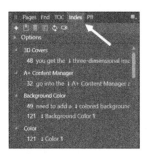

There are also menu options related to indexes under the Text option in the top menu. Go to Text->Index and you'll see the available options there, namely Insert Index Mark, Insert Index, Update Index, and Show Index Marks:

This menu is where I'd get into trouble. I was trying to use the menu option for Insert Index Mark (that shortcut was too complicated for me to actually want to use), but I would accidentally click on Insert Index instead.

Don't be me.

Also note here how Insert Index is grayed out because there's already an index in the document. That's why my workaround worked.

Alright, now that you know where everything is, let's go ahead and walk through how to insert an index into your document.

Here we have a new document where I've pasted in the appendix from my Affinity book and then applied my index master page to the last page and typed in Index into the header section I created:

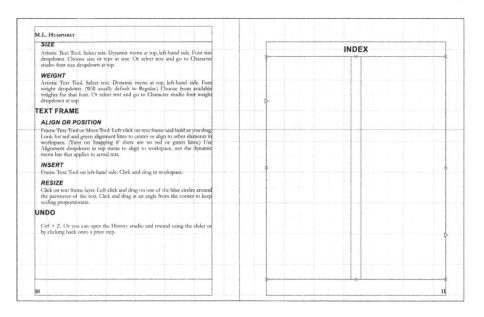

This is a master page I created specifically for use with my index, so there is no text flow from the left-hand page to the right-hand page. Also, the left-hand page has text in a single text frame while the right-hand page is using a text frame that contains two columns.

MARK AN INDEX ENTRY

The first thing I do, as mentioned above, is I flag an entry for my index. It does not matter where that entry is in my document, I just need an entry flagged.

In this case, I'm going to highlight "Text Frame" on the left-hand page and add that to my index.

There are two ways to do this.

The best one is in the Index studio. Click on the little flag for Insert Marker.

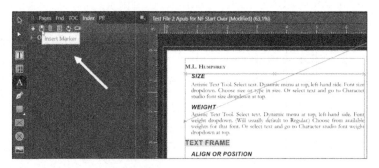

That will open the Insert Index Mark dialogue box and it should also populate the Topic Name field with the text you highlighted.

For me just now it did not populate that field so I had to type it in. But normally you should have something that looks like this:

If the Topic Name is what you want, then click OK. If it is not, change it, and then click OK. If you already have an index mark with the name you want, use the dropdown option to find it.

The other way to mark an entry is through the Text menu. Go to Text->Index and then choose Insert Index Mark from the secondary dropdown. That, too, will open the Insert Index Mark dialogue box.

Or you could use the Ctrl shortcut (Ctrl + Alt +Shift + [ ).

Even though it requires more steps to use the menu option, when Affinity was not showing me my highlighted text in my Topic Name field using the Index studio, that was still working through the menu option. So if you run into that issue you'll have to decide if you'd rather copy and paste or retype your text into the dialogue box, or go through the menu option.

Whichever method you use, when you click OK at the bottom of the dialogue box that will add the text you had in the Topic Name box into your index listing in the Index studio along with a page reference.

You don't have to highlight relevant text to generate an index marker. I sometimes will just click anywhere on a page to set a marker so that I can have my index show that X topic is covered on pages ten through fifteen.

If you don't set a marker on each of those pages it won't show it as a page range. Note also that the page range shown in the index studio is the overall page number in the document, not necessarily the page number that you see on the actual page.

For example, I had front matter in my document, so my index entry shows page 18 even though my formatted document shows that this text was on page 10.

Good news is that despite what it shows in the Index studio, when you insert your index into your document it will show the formatted document page number.

Let's do that now.

INSERT INDEX

Click into your document where you want the index to start and then go to the Index studio and click on the Insert Index option there. It's the third one after the plus sign at the top and looks like a page with some writing on it:

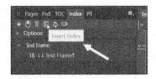

And here you can see that it inserted with page 10 for my text frame entry even though the Index studio shows it on page 18:

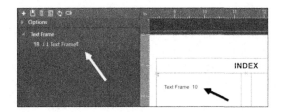

Your other option for inserting an index into your document is the top menu. Go to Text->Index->Insert Index.

UPDATE INDEX

Once you have inserted an index into your document, you can use the Update Index option under Text->Index->Update Index or go to the top of the Index studio and use the option there. It's the one with the circling arrows. Hold your mouse over it and it'll say Update Index.

At least in some versions of Affinity I found that I had to delete the index entries that were already in my document before I could update the index. But just now I wasn't required to do that, so this may be something that's no longer an issue or that only is an issue under certain circumstances.

But basically if you ever try to update your index and it doesn't work, go into your document, delete all of your index entries, and then insert the index again.

PARENT TOPICS

You can get fancier with your index by creating a hierarchy of entries using parent topics.

For example, here in my appendix of quick takes on Affinity I have Align or Position, Insert, and Resize as subcategories under Text Frame.

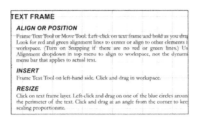

I want to keep that same hierarchy in my index.

The first step to doing so is making Text Frame into an index entry. We already did that above.

The next step is to take one of the sub-entries I want to put under Text Frame and make an index entry out of it, too. So I'm going to highlight Insert and click to insert an index marker for it.

Affinity auto-populated Topic Name for me. If I clicked on OK right now Insert would be an entry in my index at the same level as Text Frame. But I can click on the dropdown there for Parent Topic and see all of my existing entries in my index:

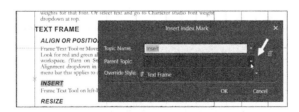

If I choose Text Frame from that dropdown, then Affinity will add Insert as an index entry but it will put that entry under the parent topic, Text Frame.

Here's what the dialogue box looks like after I make that selection:

And here's what my index looks like when I say OK:

See how Insert is indented and listed under Text Frame?

When I then update the index in my document, it is also listed under Text Frame:

Note that both entries appear under T in the index.

REMOVE PAGE NUMBERING FOR PARENT TOPIC

In the screenshot above you can see that both Text Frame and Insert show the page number for the entry. But maybe I don't want Text Frame to have the page numbers listed, too. Maybe I just want it to be a header and only worry about displaying page numbers for the sub-topics like Insert.

In that case, I can go back to the Text Frame entry in my Index studio and delete the page-specific flag I have there under Text Frame. I do so by clicking on that page number entry listed below Text Frame and then using the trash can up top.

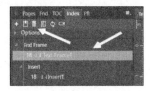

This time when I generate my index the Text Frame entry has no separate page numbering:

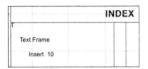

MOVE AN EXISTING ENTRY BELOW ANOTHER

Sometimes I will add an entry as a standalone index entry and later change my mind and decide it should be a subtopic instead.

Like here where I have Align or Position as its own entry and then Text Frame as a separate entry.

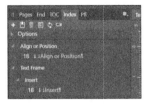

One way to fix this issue is to left-click and drag the entry you want to be a subtopic onto the entry you want as its parent topic.

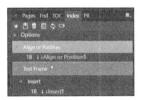

The entry you click and drag will be highlighted blue and when you're on top of the parent topic it too will be blue like you can see above. Release the left-click at that point and Affinity should automatically position the entry you moved as a sub-entry to the one you dragged it to. Like this:

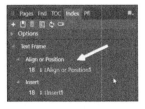

You can see that Align or Position is now indented below Text Frame.

Your other option is to right-click on the entry you want to make a sub-topic and choose to Edit Topic from the dropdown menu:

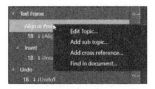

That opens an Edit Topic Index dialogue box that's identical to the dialogue box for inserting a new marker. Add a parent topic there and click OK and it will move the entry for you.

MOVE A SUB-TOPIC ENTRY TO PARENT TOPIC LEVEL

This is also how you can move an entry from being a subtopic back to being a primary topic. Right-click on the entry, choose Edit Topic, and then in the Edit Topic dialogue box click into the Parent Topic field, highlight the text that's there and delete it. You may need to then click back into the Parent Topic field so that no parent topic is selected. When your dialogue box shows your original entry but no value for the parent topic, click on OK.

That will move the entry from underneath its parent topic to its own entry.

MULTIPLE SUB-TOPIC LEVELS

You can nest a topic under more than one topic. For example, let's say I wanted Elements as a parent topic and then I wanted Insert as a sub-topic and then under that I wanted Text Frame, Picture Frame, etc.

I can do that. It works the exact same way. Build from the top down if you're going to do that. So have a topic for Elements and then create a topic for Insert with a parent of Elements. That way when you go to add your topic for Text Frame you'll have a choice in your Parent Topic dropdown that is shown as "Elements, Insert".

That comma between the words is an indicator that the parent topic has multiple levels. It will be listed alphabetically by the highest-level parent topic.

RENAME AN ENTRY

To rename a topic or fix a typo in a topic name, click on the name in the listing in the Index studio and then click on it again until the text is highlighted in blue and can be edited. Type in your updated name. Hit enter.

CROSS-REFERENCES AND ADDING ENTRIES DIRECTLY

Another thing you can do is add a cross-reference in your index.

Let's say that I want to list all of my control commands under one heading but I also want to have people be able to look for something like "Undo" in my index and still find that entry, too.

First, I'm going to add a new entry for Ctrl Commands and I don't want to flag this to one specific entry or page.

I can do so by using the + sign at the top of the Index studio. Clicking on that opens the Add Index Topic dialogue box. I can then type in my text in the Topic Name field and it will add that text as an index entry without a page reference.

Once I have that, I can take an existing index entry, in this case "Undo", and right-click on it. From the dropdown menu I can then choose Add Cross Reference.

This brings up the Add Cross-Reference dialogue box which has a dropdown menu I can select from that contains all of the entries in my index.

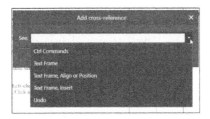

I choose Ctrl Commands and choose OK.

Now, this is not going to work yet because I have no actual entries under Ctrl Commands. The index will not update to show a manually-added entry without at least one page reference or sub-topic that has a page reference.

So I now need to create an additional entry for Undo with a parent topic of Ctrl Commands.

Or, if I don't care about listing the page number under my Undo listing, I could just move my existing page reference from Undo up to Ctrl Commands. Which is what I did here:

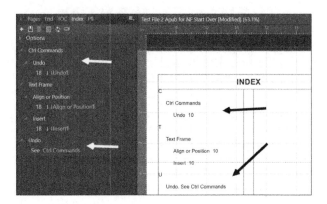

Note how the index under Undo says, "See Ctrl Commands" and there's an entry for Undo under Ctrl Commands with a page number?

You also don't actually have to have overlapping words like that. You can have a cross-reference from Add to Insert, for example, and that would work just as well. All you need is an actual entry under the one being referenced or it won't show in your index.

MANUAL UPDATES

That's the basics of working with an index.

Once your index is inserted into your document it can be edited just like any other text in your document. I will, for example, sometimes combine the entries for letters like U through Z to take up less space.

But remember, just like with the table of contents, because Affinity generates your index for you, if you do make manual edits to your index and then regenerate that index for any reason you will lose those edits.

TEXT STYLE UPDATES

The index does use text styles so you can always edit the formatting of your text and then update that text style if you want to apply that formatting to all of your entries.

OTHER THOUGHTS

What else?

There is a setting there at the top of the Index studio to have it show your index markers for you. I've never used it myself. I basically get everything in the book finalized and then go through from page one to the end and mark things as I see them and then that's it.

Also, sometimes I will use the same sub-topic in a document. So I might have "Insert" under multiple parent categories. This is absolutely doable, but there have been times when Affinity really wanted to use the existing Parent Topic and I needed to click away from choosing that parent topic or get it back to a blank parent topic before I could assign the sub-topic to a new parent topic.

So know it is possible, it just may take a little work to get it right.

That's basically it.

As I mentioned before, you can only have one index in a document.

Nice thing, though, is that if you're merging multiple documents into one, the markers you set in each of those documents will feed into that single index, so you don't have to redo all of that work when you merge documents.

So let's talk about that next, how to merge multiple documents into one. It's another fiddly one but definitely useful to master.

MERGE MULTIPLE BOOKS INTO ONE TITLE

I generally take any series of books I've written and publish it as a collection or omnibus when it's done. So the *Excel Essentials* series, for example, has *Excel for Beginners, Intermediate Excel, 50 Useful Excel Functions,* and *50 More Excel Functions* available as standalone titles but it also has *Excel Essentials* available for purchase. (That thing is a behemoth. It's an inch thick.)

The only time I don't do this is when the book is too massive when combined or when the individual titles were never really meant to be a collection like that. For example, my Easy Excel Essentials series are all meant to be one-off titles for a specific purpose because ideally someone would just buy the Excel Essentials books if they needed more than that.

(Not that people always act in the ways I expect.)

Anyway. Combining multiple books in Affinity is something you will also likely want to do at some point, either for fiction or non-fiction, so it's definitely worth covering. But it can be a lot of fiddly work, so I'm actually going to start with a fiction example which is much simpler to handle and then move on to a non-fiction example after that.

And so I don't forget anything I'm going to work through both examples with real files that need to be combined. It may make things a little longer, but at least there won't be some obvious step I forget.

First up is combining three of my cozy mystery books. I publish these books as standalones but also publish every three books as a collection and right now I have a short story and two of the books for the next collection ready to go so it's a perfect example to use.

I always work off of the file for the first book, so that's step one, open that book in Affinity.

The way I have my collections set up is I have a title page for the collection, a copyright and Also By page for the collection after that, and then a table of contents for the collection.

For my fiction collections I then have a page that has a black and white version of the book cover for the first title and then the copyright information and the text of the first title. I do the same for all of the other books in the collection.

My next step then is to figure out what material I can scavenge from the original file for the first book.

It starts with a title page that I can convert to a title page for the collection.

I can also use the Also By page as-is as well as the pages I have with the book cover, copyright notice, and main body text:

The About the Author at the end will have to go. I'll pull that from the last book I add.

Now that I know what to repurpose, what to keep, and what I need to add I can go to the first page of my document and change the title to the one for the collection.

To do so I click on the Artistic Text Tool (the capital A), go to the first page, and make my changes to the text. Ideally that's all you should have to do.

In my case I had to do more because the text wasn't wrapped around the image, but it needed to be. So that required me to go to the master page and fix that setting.

On the next two-page spread I was able to keep the Also By section on the right-hand page as-is, but I needed to add text for the collection copyright.

I had a choice to either do so on the master page or the actual page in the document. I went ahead and did so in the document itself.

So I clicked and dragged a text frame into place, copied my text from the individual title's copyright page, and pasted it into the frame.

(This has the added benefit of giving me the earliest copyright year I need if I choose to just have one copyright notice, but since I'm leaving the individual copyright notices after their title pages, I'll just do one for the collection.)

I updated the copyright notice to include the word Collection before the word Copyright and XXX'ed out the current ISBN. I'll update that when I'm ready to provide one for the collection, but in the meantime those XXX's should be flagged as a spelling error in preflight so I won't forget to update it.

I also changed the copyright year to this one.

Here we are so far:

In the original document the next page is the page with the cover image, but I need a new page before that with the table of contents for the collection.

I can do that with a right-click and Add Pages selection from the dropdown menu which will bring up the Add Pages dialogue box.

I can either right-click on the Also By page spread and choose to insert the new spread "after" or I can right-click on the book cover image page spread and choose to insert "before". (I could also technically insert anywhere I want and drag the page spread into place, but why add the extra step?)

The master page I use for this is the Simple Title Page, which is the same one I used for page 1.

For now because we don't have the other titles in the document yet, this page is just going to be a placeholder page. Once we have all of the books in I'll need to circle back and either insert a table of contents on this page or manually enter a table of contents. (Not a best practice to manually enter the text, but it looks like that's what I've done with the prior collections for these books. Shame on me.)

Because I know I have that issue I went ahead and at least listed table of contents and the book titles.

After that the next umpteen pages get to be left just as they are because this is the first book and it should be set up to just flow from there.

I do need to check the first page of the first chapter to be sure it starts on page 1, but it should be fine.

And here we are with the rest of the front matter:

Next step is to go to the end of the document and delete anything from the back matter. In my case that's just the final page spread which has my about the author page.

In my fantasy series that would include the character and term listings, because those would need to move to the end of the collection and I'd just use the one from the last book in the series.

Also, sometimes I will have a little "read the next book" note at the end of my last chapter. That text needs to be deleted as well.

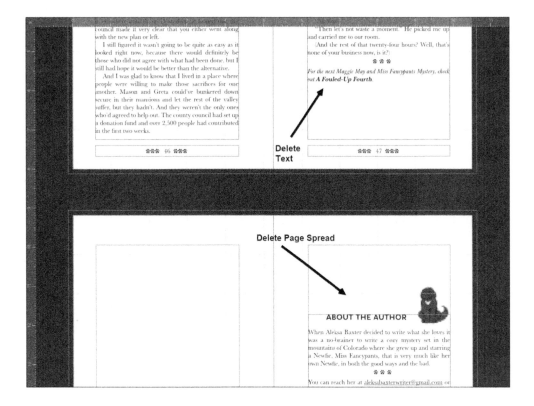

One thing to watch out for when you delete any back matter pages or text at the end of the book is red circles around the text frame. Like this:

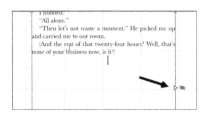

That indicates an overflowing text frame. And what that means in this particular instance is that my "About the Author" text was text that was flowing from my main body text.

Sometimes I set my books up that way, sometimes my about the author text is separate.

If the text were separate I could have deleted those two pages and been done. But because my text is flowing from my main body to that About the Author page the text was not actually deleted when I deleted those two pages.

I have two options for fixing this. I can undo back to before I deleted the pages at the end of the document, delete the text on those pages, and then delete the pages again.

Or I can click at the very end of my main body text and start using the Delete key until I've pulled the text back onto that page where I can then delete it.

I went with the undo option. That way I know I got it all and I'm not stuck in some annoying loop of trying to delete text I can't actually see until I delete it.

When you're done, you want that last page spread to be the end of your first title.

One more thing to do before we move on and bring in the second title. You can technically wait to do this until the end but I'm going to do it now because it'll throw me otherwise.

Right now, because this is a fiction title, my headers are pulling in the book title. But to have this work when it's a collection I need to swap that over to section names and then assign each book to its own section.

To do so, I first go back to the Master Pages section, find any page that has the book title in the header and swap that out for the Section Name field.

In this case I have the Chapter Start and Text master page as well as the Text and Text master page to fix.

Remember you do this by highlighting the book title, deleting it, and then going to Text->Insert->Fields->Section Name.

Once that's done, go to the first page of Chapter 1, right-click, Start New Section, and name that section for the first title in your collection.

Now it's time to bring in the next book.

This is where it gets wacky. Because even though in a standalone title the first page starts on the right-hand side, that's not how it works when you add that file onto the end of another one.

Affinity also does not treat that first page spread as a two-page spread. Which means that unless you prep your file properly the first page of the next book will come in on the left-hand side and all of your pages will be off by one. Everything that should be on the right will be on the left, and vice versa.

To not have this problem, what I'm going to do is go to the end of my current document and insert a two-page spread.

I want one that has a blank left-hand page. It really doesn't matter which one I choose as long as that left-hand page is blank.

Next, I'm going to right-click on the right-hand page of that spread and delete that right-hand page.

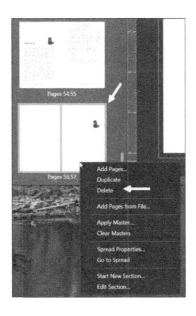

Note that I am only deleting the right-hand page. See that the blue outline is only around that page, not the page spread.

Doing this leaves me with a document that has a blank page at the end on the left-hand side. Which means when I bring in my next file, the next place to put a page will be on the right-hand side and all of my pages will be in the appropriate place.

To do that, I right-click on that last page and choose Add Pages from File from the dropdown:

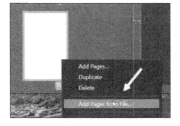

That will open a dialogue box where I can navigate to the second book file and choose Open. At that point Affinity will show the Add Pages dialogue box.

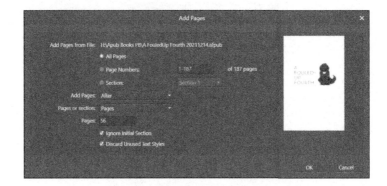

I want All Pages, After, Pages, and my last page number which in this case is 56.

I tried this both with and without Ignore Initial Section checked and it didn't make any difference that I could see.

For some odd reason it brought my first page in without text, but since we're going to delete it, that's fine.

I now have three page spreads at the beginning of my second title that look like this:

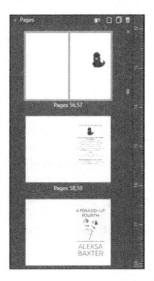

The page there at the top with the blue outline is the last page from our first file that we inserted. The page next to it is the title page for my second title and then the rest of the pages you see are the ones that flow from there.

Every once in a while when you try to bring in another book you may run into a situation where there is an Imported Text Styles dialogue box that appears. This won't always happen, but it definitely can. That generally means there's some sort of conflict or overlap between the styles used in the two documents.

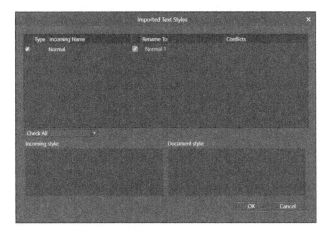

For example here I probably for some reason have a style in each file named Normal. If I don't want to change any of my text formatting I can just click the Rename To box and that will keep both text styles in the document and rename the one for the imported file to Normal 1 so the two styles don't have the same name anymore.

That's usually what I do. I can then scan the document later for any big differences and fix them at that point with a find and replace for text style or by manually applying the text style I want. But at the import stage I like to just leave things alone.

Okay, back to our file with the newly-imported second book.

Because this is the second title in the collection I don't need the same front matter. I can have this section start with the book cover, which means I can delete the first two page spreads, the one with the title page and the one with the also by text.

Next, I need to set a section start on the page for chapter 1 of this second book and give that section the book's name. I also want to make sure to continue numbering because you don't start page numbering over with a collection:

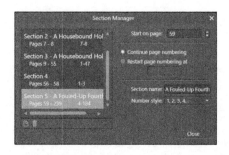

But in this case I need to continue numbering for the prior section, too, which covers the two blank pages before chapter one of the second book starts as well as the page with the book cover image.

You can see that was a problem in the image above because Section 4 is showing 1-3 in the right-hand side of its listing but it should be showing 48-50 because it should be continuing the numbering of the prior section like Section 5 is currently doing. (Section 5 shows page 59-239 on the left-hand side which represent the overall pages in the document contained in the section but 4-184 on the right-hand side because it is continuing the page numbering from Section 4.)

If that sounds confusing, don't worry about it. You'll see in the document itself that your numbers are off and know you need to fix them. You can even save that for the very end if you want when you scan through the whole thing.

Okay.

Next step is to go to the end of the newly-merged document and delete any back matter. Keep going through those steps for each book you want to include until you reach the last one.

When you reach the final file, don't delete the back matter like you did with the other files you brought in. Instead, see which parts of the back matter to keep. In this case I just have an about the author page, so that definitely stays.

The next step is to do a scan through and review to make sure everything landed where it should, that your page numbers are continuous from the first title through, and that your headers reflect the correct book.

You can generate a PDF at this point and review that or just scroll up and down and view the pages on your screen. If you do export to PDF this is a good time to export as All Spreads because then the pages will export as a pair with the left-hand page on the left-hand side and the right-hand page on the right-hand side of the spread so it's easier to review that the content is on the correct side of the page.

(You can't submit an All Spreads export to KDP or IngramSpark, but it is handy for document review.)

The final step is the table of contents. Best to finalize that when everything else in the document is as it should be.

In this case, I'd been doing these manually which is not a best practice. What I can do instead since I don't have a title page to pull my titles from, is insert a text frame layer behind the cover images for each of my titles. That will hide that layer during the export. I can then add my title to that hidden text frame, assign a book title text style to it, and use that book title style to generate my table of contents.

That works. Affinity generates a table of contents for me, shows the start page for each book as the page with the cover image on it, and on those cover image pages I don't see the text in that hidden text frame.

Done. Now on to the harder example, a non-fiction collection.

* * *

I'm going to create a collection using the first three Affinity books.

First step then is to open *Affinity Publisher for Fiction Layouts*.

The front matter we want for the collection is going to be very similar to that we had for fiction.

I want a collection title page, collection copyright, an also by page, an overarching table of contents and then an individual book title page, individual book copyright page, individual book table of contents, and individual book content.

At the end I want any relevant appendix that applies across the books as well as an index for all the titles.

To make this happen, I need to insert two new page spreads, one for the first book's title page and one for the overarching table of contents. Since they use different master page layouts I inserted them one at a time but I could have inserted them both at once and then just changed the master page style for one or the other.

My next step is to copy the text from the first page, which contains my original title page text, and paste that into my newly-inserted master page that will be for the first book's title page.

I do it this way, because that first page spread is a little funky since it's only a right-hand page and I don't want to deal with whatever complications inserting a master page at the start might create. So better to copy and paste the text from that page and then type over the existing text on that first page to create my collection title page.

That's what I do next.

I do the copyright notice after that. In this case, I copy the copyright text for the individual title and paste it into an inserted text frame that I place right before the page for the collection table of contents. I then edit that copyright notice to pertain to the collection.

For now we're going to leave the table of contents page empty.

So here are our first five pages. We have the collection title page, the collection copyright, the also by, a blank page, and then the table of contents for the collection:

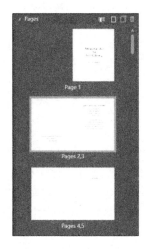

After those five pages, we have the beginning of the first book which contains its title page, copyright notice, and table of contents:

So far this is very similar to what we did for the cozy mystery collection, but now things change.

First, I do not have to create any sections this time. That's because I already had sections since I was using chapter titles for my headers.

Second, this book has its own table of contents so that's going to require some adjustments.

Look at the last four items that are currently in that table of contents:

CONTENTS (CONT.)

Chapter Start and Text Master Page	119
Fix Missing Italics or Bolded Text	123
Assign a Page One	125
Tidy Up	129
Add Back Matter	131
Text and No Text Master Page	133
No Text and Section Start Master Page	135
Finalize Back Matter	137
Preflight	139
Export a PDF	141
Reuse an Old Book	145
Conclusion	147
Appendix A: Quick Takes	149
Appendix B: Create a Book From An Existing FILE	157
Index	159
About the Author	165

There are two appendices, an index, and an about the author page. All of those should be part of the collection, not part of this individual title. Which means this table of contents will need updated at some point after we delete those sections.

Also, to make my life difficult, the quick takes in this first book here are not the same as the ones for the ads and book covers titles which are books two and three in the collection. Very different tasks involved between print formatting and image manipulation.

So I need to make a choice. Do I integrate the two quick takes appendices into one large quick takes appendix? Or keep them separate?

I think I'm going to try to keep them separate. For now, though, I can just delete this.

So my next step is to go to the end of the present document and delete those four sections. I want to delete the contents of the index, though, before I delete the pages it is on.

To do so, I go to the index section, click into that text frame with my index contents, use Ctrl + A to select all of my index entries, and then use the Delete key.

I also need to individually delete the "Index" text at the top of that page. Otherwise it may end up somewhere weird when I delete that page.

Now I can delete all of the back matter pages.

I end up with a final page on the left-hand side that has text on it. Which means I need a blank page on the right-hand side to match that page as well as one additional blank page by itself on the left-hand side after that.

When I try to apply a text and no text master page to that last page to add my right-hand blank page, nothing happens. It just stays a single standalone page. If I had a no text and no text master page, I could just insert it here, but I don't.

What I can do, though, is insert a no text and chapter start master page, and then go to the newly orphaned last page that is a chapter start page and change its assigned master page style to a no text and text master page style.

It's an awkward way for me to get two blank pages in a row like that, but it does seem to work.

Now that I have that blank left-hand page by itself I can bring in the second book using the Add Pages from File option and know that the pages will fall where they should.

This one had a lot of Imported Text Styles it wanted to show me:

But since there are no conflicts listed, I'm just going to click on OK. That

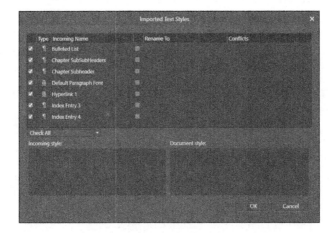

means both documents will use the same text styles.

Each one should be the same style with the same formatting, and they came in fine as far as I can tell right now.

I tested it with a quick search for any text with one of the styles using the Find option and then scrolled down until I found an image in that same section to confirm it didn't accidentally shift the text due to a formatting change.

It looks like there was no impact. And there really shouldn't have been because I created book two using the file from book one. (I am lazy so I just open the last book in the series, delete the main body content from that last book, and then drop in the next book's content when I'm ready to do the next book in a series.) It would only be a problem if I'd for some reason changed that style in book two. But then Affinity should've told me there was a conflict, which it did not.

(Always do a final pass of your document, though.)

Okay.

Next I need to move the copyright notice for this book to the page spread with the table of contents specific to book two and then I can delete the Also By page spread.

After that, I can go to the end of the newly-merged document and delete book two's back matter.

And that crashed my file.

If that happens to you, don't panic. Open Affinity again and you should see a message like this:

I always say Yes.

Now you get to find out how much you lost and also, if you're me, cuss at yourself for not saving a version of the file yet.

So first step is to save the file under the name you actually wanted to use for it if you're me.

Second step is to see what you lost. Fortunately, my answer is nothing. It saved right up until the pages I tried to delete that it didn't like me deleting. Which is usually the case with Affinity. I have definitely had it crash on me, but do not recall losing a significant amount of edits when that happened.

Which leaves us with a choice to make.

Do we assume the crash was a one-off error and try to delete those same pages again, possibly risking crashing the program a second time? Or do we take a more measured approach?

I'm going to assume it's my index giving me issues, which means it'll do it again.

So I'm going to do a Ctrl + A in my index section and delete the text of the index before I try to delete my pages.

This time it did not crash. Yay!

Now that those pages are gone I can add two blank pages at the end like I did before and insert my final file. (For now. In reality this book I'm writing right now will be the final file. But we'll pretend.)

This time I did have a conflict in the Imported Text Styles:

I can leave it like this and it will change the bulleted list style for one of the two

books, or I can check that Rename To box and let it bring the bulleted list style used in the third book as a new style.

I'm going to check the box. I have too many images in these books to mess up any of my spacing. (You'll understand better why that's an issue for me when we cover image placement in the next chapter.)

Okay.

Same process with the front matter. Move the copyright notice, delete the also by page.

Now we have to deal with the Appendices and the Index. This is the last table of contents in the document, so if we don't change the text style assigned to the Appendix, the Index, and the About the Author sections to something different from our chapter titles, then the table of contents for book three will include them like it is currently:

We don't want that.

CONTENTS

Introduction 1
Design Principles 3
Ebook Cover with a Central Image 9
Ebook Cover with a Side Image 33
Ebook Cover with a Single Image for the Entire Cover 49
KDP Paperback Cover 61
IngramSpark Paperback Cover 77
IngramSpark Case Laminate Hard Cover 87
Conclusion 95
Appendix A: Affinity Publisher Quick Takes 99
Index 109
About the Author 115

So let's go to the Appendix now. We have a choice to make. We can continue to have the Appendix formatted the exact same way as before but just assign it a new style name. Or we can change the formatting and assign that its own name.

I'm lazy, so I'm going to just create a new style but not make any formatting changes. Which means we can click onto the Appendix title row and then go up to the Text Style dropdown menu and choose New Style from there and give the text style its own name.

It is unchanged and identical looking to the chapter style, but now we can

differentiate the two for table of contents purposes.

Next I need to go through and apply that new style to any other back matter headers I have. Easy enough.

And now the annoying bits.

First, I have two appendices from the first book that I need to bring back in. (Let me pause to save my file real quick…)

The first of those appendices was eight pages long. I'm going to click onto the last main page of my third book and insert eight pages with a text and text master page format using the Add Pages option in the dropdown menu.

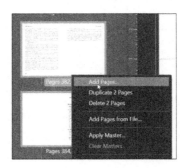

Once the pages are inserted I can go to the first set of inserted pages and change the master page format to a no text and section start master page.

I'm now going to go back to the first file, copy the text for that first Appendix and paste the text into this page. The text does not automatically flow to the next page, but good news is it also doesn't end up back in the main body of my third book.

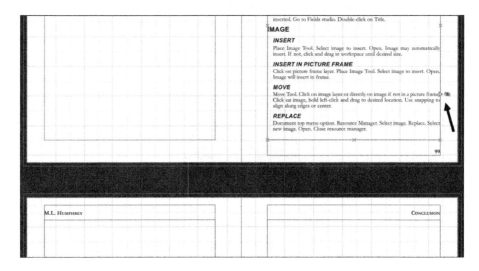

Because I have content past this inserted section, I can't have Affinity auto-flow the appendix text for me. So I need to click on that red triangle and then click in my text frame on the left-hand side frame on the next page and keep doing that for all of the pages of this appendix to get the text to flow through.

After I've done that I can go back to the appendix header, apply my new back matter text style, and also change the name since I'm going to have two quick takes appendices.

I can now change the name for the second quick takes appendix as well, making it Appendix B and specific to images.

I decided to put the other appendix from the first book behind the quick takes appendices. It's the same process of adding pages for the text and then bringing in the text and flowing it through.

Now it's time to tackle the Index.

But, actually, it isn't. Because I want my page numbers behaving before I do this and I don't think they are. Actually, I know they aren't. Not unless three books plus appendices are 118 total pages.

To figure out where my issue is, I right-click on a page spread in the Pages studio and choose Edit Section to bring up the Section Manager. Once I have the Section Manager open I can go through my sections after that first introduction chapter and see where I need to tell Affinity to continue numbering.

It sounds worse than it is because the only sections that should be giving me a problem are the title page or table of contents or introduction pages for each book. It won't be every single section that needs updating since those were already set up appropriately when I created the original books.

While I'm at it, I should assign sections to the two appendices I pasted into the document manually.

Okay, so once that's done and I'm comfortable that the page numbering throughout the whole document is working properly (238 pages is much more like it), I can finally tackle the Index. Here's the first page:

You can see that there are already entries there. But I'm not sure this index is pulling in entries from all three books.

To be sure, I need to refresh the index. Let me see if the Update option will work.

I go to the Index studio and click on the arrows at the top for Update and, yes, it worked. (If that didn't work I would've just deleted the index entries I could see in the document and then used the Insert option instead.)

Because this is now an index with entries for three books instead of one, I have more text than available space as you can see from the red arrows around the text frames:

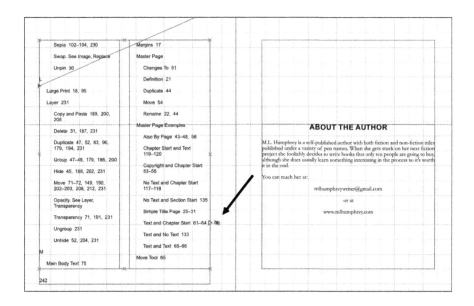

That means I need to go back to the Pages studio, insert some new pages between that index page and my about the author page, assign the proper master pages to them, and then flow my text to get the whole index visible.

And I realized as I did that I must've missed one "continue numbering" option with my pages because I have 414 pages showing on the left-hand side in the Pages studio but my document is only showing 250 or so pages.

So I have to fix that, too, and then update the index one more time. Fortunately, it's pretty easy to know when you've messed up and find the fix. Unfortunately, I don't think I've ever done one of these books where there wasn't something that I missed the first time through.

It happens, so prepare for that and check, recheck, and check again.

The easiest way to find where that happened is to scroll back through the pages in my workspace until I see a page 1. My Pages studio will roughly keep pace as I do so, which means when I get to that point I can then right-click on the correct page spread in the Pages studio, Edit Section, and update that section to continue numbering.

Here's the culprit. I have a page 1 in my layout but it's page 167 of my overall document:

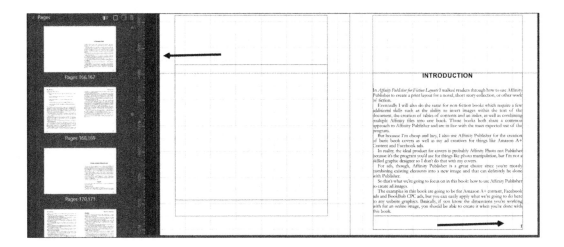

So time to right-click, Edit Section, and fix it. Just make sure that you're making your changes to that actual section and not a different one. (Like I almost did just now…)

Finally it's time to deal with our tables of contents. Remember, we have four of them—the overarching one that will list our book titles and back matter and then the three individual ones that will list the chapters for each book.

It's probably easier to do the back three before we do the front one, but we can also take care of a few things along the way that will help with the main table of contents.

So I'm going to go back to the start of the document and scroll down until I see my first title page that isn't the collection title page. I click on that title and note the text style used. In my case it's Book Title. I'll need that later for my main table of contents.

I keep going to the next page which has the table of contents for this specific book. I click into the document where the TOC text is and then look at the TOC studio.

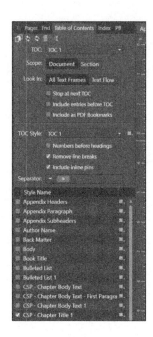

(Now's when I hope I didn't do a lot of manual formatting to any of my tables of contents.)

The first thing I need to do for this table of contents is check the "Stop at next TOC" box. That's going to update my table of contents so that it stops pulling entries when it reaches book two.

The next thing I need to do is see if it looks okay now. How's the formatting? Any weird page-numbering issues? Any weird text entries? Any text overflow? There shouldn't be, but if it turns out I manually adjusted things, there could be.

Also, I need to make sure that the last entry in this table of contents is the last chapter in this particular book and that it's no longer pulling in the appendices, about the author, or other back matter sections.

(Sometimes even though you deleted the pages that had those sections on them the headers can get caught somewhere in the ether and be hanging out behind the scenes and they'll show up in your table of contents entries. This usually happens if the text flowed from the last chapter straight into the back matter instead of those being completely separate sections of your document.)

So let's look:

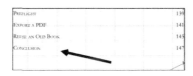

Preflight	139
Export a PDF	141
Reuse an Old Book	145
Conclusion	147

All good. The last entry listed is the Conclusion just as it should be.

On to the next.

I locate the next table of contents, click into it, change the TOC dropdown to TOC 2 in the Table of Contents studio, check the box for stop at next TOC, and then verify that it too looks okay.

Here's that dropdown:

If you don't change the dropdown to the next TOC even though you're clicked onto it all of the settings will still be for that first table of contents, and when you click on Update it will update the first table of contents not the one you're clicked on.

(Ask me how I know…)

This one looks good, too, so on to the third one. Same process.

Except when I updated my third table of contents my first table of contents pulled in the entries from my second table of contents and wouldn't refresh to get rid of them.

I obviously could've been messing something up somewhere, but the only solution I found that worked was to delete that first table of contents and re-insert it. Of course, that required me to reformat my table of content entries because it was a new table of contents.

Good times.

Okay. Once you've sorted your interior tables of contents, it's time to insert the main, overarching table of contents.

I go back to that blank fifth page of my document, click into the text frame for where I want to insert the table of contents, and then go to the Table of Contents studio and click on the Insert option:

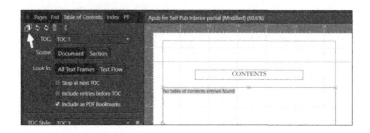

Hopefully it defaults to no entries found like this one did so you can just go check the boxes for the styles you need. I know that I want to use Book Title and Back Matter to flag my entries based on what I noted down previously. When I do that I get this result:

That is very ugly.

And it's going to require some manual adjustment on my part to fix because I had line breaks on my title pages. But let's save that for last.

First, I need to go back to the Tables of Contents studio and for each style I need to tell it to include page numbers.

Next, I need to highlight one of the lines of text and change the formatting to what I want. I'm going to use Garamond, 16 pt, small caps. I update the text style so all of the entries for that style update and then go do the same for the other entries under the second text style.

Which gets me this:

CONTENTS

Affinity Publisher	7
for	7
Fiction Layouts	7
Affinity Publisher	151
for	151
Ad Creatives	151
Affinity Publisher	271
for	271
Basic Book Covers	271
Appendix A: Print Layout Quick Takes	373
Appendix B: Image and Design Quick Takes	381
Appendix C: Create A Book From An Existing FILE	391
INDEX	393
About the Author	403

I now have two choices. I can go to the title pages for each book and remove those line breaks and just let the text flow as it will. That will let this table of contents update automatically without needing manual adjustments. Or I can remove those line breaks here on the page, but the next time I update this table of contents I'll have to fix it again. (And I know I'll have to update the table of contents again because I still need to add in this book I'm writing right now.)

Also, I always forget about the difference in appearance between INDEX and Index when I'm using small caps. See how that stands out atrociously? Same with the word FILE.

So I need to go adjust that text, too, to make it upper and lower case.

I went to that first title page, removed the line breaks, and decided it worked just fine so did that to the other two and then made my edits to file and index and here we go:

CONTENTS

Affinity Publisher for Fiction Layouts	7
Affinity Publisher for Ad Creatives	151
Affinity Publisher for Basic Book Covers	271
Appendix A: Print Layout Quick Takes	373
Appendix B: Image and Design Quick Takes	381
Appendix C: Create A Book From An Existing File	391
Index	393
About the Author	403

Much, much better.

Although that B in Appendix B still needs fixed. Looks like it's lower-case right now.

And I might want to change my formatting so that the back matter is somehow set apart from the three main book titles, but for now, we're good.

If this were the final version of this book I'd now need to generate my PDF and scan through the whole thing making sure that page starts fall where they should and that all images imported properly and that nothing moved around.

I'd also want to see that my headers still make sense and double-check my page numbering.

It's a lot of work to merge non-fiction books in Affinity, but it's a helluva lot better to do it this way than have to go through and re-place 100+ images per book and add markers for a new index.

Speaking of images, let's talk about image placement and adjustment next.

IMAGE PLACEMENT

I saved image placement for last because I wanted to be sure I delivered value before diving in on this topic.

Now, don't get me wrong, I have a lot of experience placing images in Affinity documents. Each of these books has around a hundred different screenshots and at this point I've done over a dozen image-heavy books between the Excel, Word, Access, PowerPoint, and Affinity titles.

And, yes, they have turned out okay. If you're reading this in print and you've reached this point then I have to assume you didn't yet throw the book across the room because you couldn't read the images.

But. (There's always a but.) I don't think that the way I place images in Affinity is the way you're really supposed to do it.

Because I use picture frames to place my images. I did this initially because I wanted every image I placed to have a border around it and that was the easiest way I could find to make that happen. Also, I found it easier to center my images using a picture frame.

It does also let me control which part of an image is visible on the page, but that's generally not something that's an issue since I want the images I use in the print version and the ebook version to be the same. I think maybe half a dozen times I've not shown the full image in the print version simply because it wasn't truly necessary and making the image smaller helped with formatting the page.

So I like using picture frames and will continue to do so.

The issue with my approach is that the images I insert are not anchored to the text around them. So if you were to go into one of my books and add a new paragraph at the start of a chapter, all of the text would move, but the images wouldn't. The images are fixed to that location on that page where I placed them.

Since I bring in a final product for formatting in Affinity, this isn't something that causes me a problem. But if you're going to be doing a lot of editing within the file after you place your images, then you may not want to use my approach.

You can instead pin an image to text in your document and when that text moves it will take the image along with it.

I suspect that's probably the better approach. I'm just a person who finds something that works "good enough" for me and then moves forward and the picture frame approach was that solution.

I'll cover both here, though. And I will show you how to place a border directly on your image and use the pinning settings to center it. So really the only difference between the two when we're done will be if you want to crop out part of a larger image.

Also, you'll notice in my books that I always have the image on its own line, but we'll cover how to flow text around an image instead if that's what you prefer.

Okay. Now that the disclaimers are done, let's dive in.

IMAGE QUALITY

The first topic we need to cover does not actually involve using Affinity. And that is image quality.

For print you want all of your images in your book to be 300 DPI or higher for grayscale and 600 DPI for pure black and white images (like line drawings).

And for black and white print books your color should be set to be grayscale. For IngramSpark they recommended Gray/8 last time I checked.

If you upload a file to IngramSpark that has images in it that are not at least 300 DPI (they use ppi in their guidelines but they're basically the same), they will give you an alert message.

You can override the message and they will still publish your book, but the images in your book may be blurry. Or at least blurrier than they need to be.

I will confess that the first *Excel for Beginners* edition I ever published had images that were under 300 DPI. They were still legible, but they were not as crisp as in later editions.

It was actually trying to solve this issue that led me to using Affinity, because Affinity will tell me when my images are not a high enough DPI, which is so so nice to have.

It turned out I had a multi-pronged problem. One was that I was using Word which by default compresses images. Two was that the built-in Save As PDF feature in Word also did something behind the scenes that reduced image quality, so I had to have the Adobe website convert my files for me instead. And the third prong of my problem was that I didn't have a good enough monitor to take the pictures in the first place.

It turns out that the default monitor on most laptops is simply not a high enough resolution to take images that you can use in a print book. At least, not if you want them to be any sort of reasonable size. I'd had hopes that I could connect to my TV and do it that way, but it turns out the resolution on a big television is not necessarily higher than a laptop screen.

Ultimately I had to buy a monitor that was the highest resolution I could find and that finally let me have 300 DPI images that were also large enough for a print book. (With ebooks this is not an issue because ebooks tend to only require 72 DPI or higher. That's also why you can't see this issue until you print out your images.)

Now, there are tricks you can play to make an image 300 DPI, but don't. If you take an initially 100 DPI image and make it 300 DPI it will still be just as blurry as when it was 100 DPI.

Your best bet for a good image is to take it with a high quality monitor or camera to begin with.

Okay, now that we've covered that. Let's walk through placing some images.

IMAGE PLACEMENT

While I'm writing my first draft I take my screenshots and I put a note in the text to indicate that there's an image that needs to be inserted at that spot.

This means when I paste in my text to Affinity I can then work through the document, formatting my text and placing my images as I go.

Here, for example, is the beginning of a chapter of the Affinity for covers book:

You can see that I need to insert three images here. Images 3, 4, and 5.

(I also try to number the images as I go through so that they're in order in the file where I save them, but I almost invariably end up adding text somewhere in the document and then end up with images numbered things like 3a, 3b, 3c etc. to keep them in order.)

So once I've formatted that text at the start of the chapter my next step is to insert a picture frame. I go to the left-hand menu, click on the Picture Frame Rectangle Tool, and then place a rectangle in my document at about the place where I have my note that an image should be inserted.

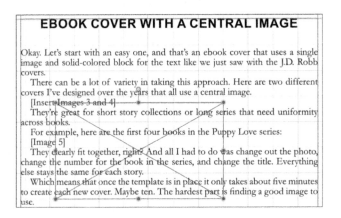

You can see that the frame when I insert it is on top of my text. I don't want that, so what I then do is go to the menu up top and click on the Show Text Wrap Settings option and choose Jump from the Wrap Style.

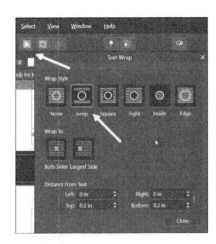

If you didn't want your image to be on its own line, this is where you could choose square or tight instead and have the text wrap either on both sides or the largest side. But as you've seen in the print version of this book and as I mentioned before, I always use jump so the image is by itself, like this:

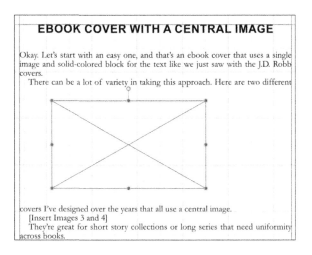

You can see that it's not quite in the correct place. It needs to move down a bit, and I could click and drag on that frame and pull it down right now so that the line of text that ends with "a central image" is above the frame, but I'm not going to.

First I want to bring in my picture, because right now I have no idea what the actual size of the image I'm bringing in is. This picture frame is not going to stay this size. And if I'm going to have to position the frame to center it when I'm done placing the image, I might as well wait to move the picture frame down until then.

Okay. So next step is to go to the Place Image Tool and bring that image in.

Usually when I bring an image in it tries to place it in the picture frame, but I accidentally changed my settings recently so that my images have started coming in at the top left of the page and at the DPI for my document, in this case 300. Which means I insert the image and then can't see it anywhere on the page.

If this happens to you, the way to find the image is to go to your Layers studio, expand the picture frame layer, and click on the image layer below it. That should place a blue border around the image like you're seeing here in the top left corner of the page spread:

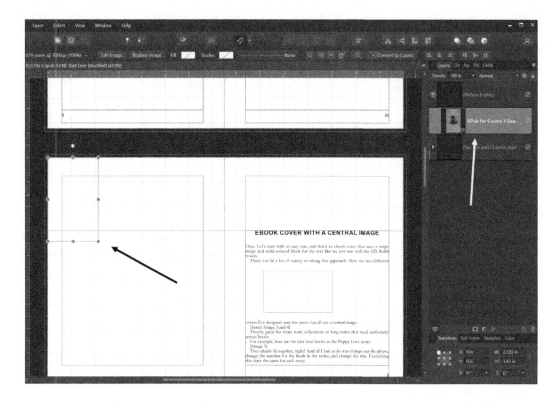

The image itself is not visible because it's inserted in a picture frame but no part of the image overlaps with the picture frame right now.

If clicking on the image layer doesn't work to make its outline visible, then go to the Transform studio and change the X or Y value for the layer to bring it to where the picture frame is or at least within the perimeter of your canvas.

Since I can see it, I click and drag it into place in the picture frame.

As I mentioned above, the nice thing about the image importing this way is that Affinity brings it in at my specified minimum DPI. That can be very helpful if you have smaller images that you're working with because you will know that the image you imported cannot be bigger than that imported size without dropping below your desired DPI.

You can also be assured that if you make that image smaller, it will still be okay. Here, for example, the image came into my picture frame at 300 DPI, but I don't need it to be that big. See that blue outline and how much space it takes up:

You can always see the image DPI in the Resource Manager:

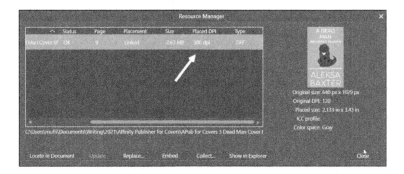

To adjust the image size, I use the Transform studio. That lets me be certain that I'll keep the image proportionate as I change its size.

To do so, I click on the image layer in the Layers studio and then go to the Transform studio and click on the Lock Aspect Ratio setting to the right of the W and H values.

I then change either W or H to what I want. If I drew the picture frame at the approximate size I wanted to use already I can use that H value or I can just guess based on the current size of the image in the document and how much I want to make the image smaller

As you decrease your image size, the DPI will go up. See here where my DPI is now 512:

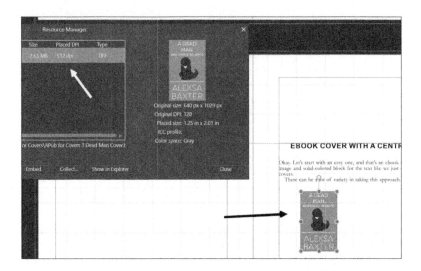

Now that the image is the size I want it to be, I need to also change my picture frame to match.

To do so, click on the picture frame layer, go to the dynamic menu up top, and click on the Size Frame to Content option.

That will both align the frame with the image and make them the same size.

Once you have your image sized and aligned inside your picture frame, it's time to position the frame relative to the text.

Go to the Layers studio and click onto the picture frame layer. Next, click onto the picture frame in your document and drag the image and frame into place.

Always be certain that you are positioning the picture frame layer not the image layer. The image moves with the frame so positioning the picture frame places them both. But if you position the image it will leave the picture frame behind and you'll then have to get the image centered on the frame once more before you position the frame.

In my case, I need to drag the frame down a little to move that one line of text up. I also want it centered.

When centering an image in a book you need to make sure that you use the correct center line, because Affinity will show you two of them. One line centers the image across the entire page, which includes the uneven margins, and one centers the image within the text frame.

You want to center within the text frame.

I believe that correct center line is always going to be the outer line, but I just do it visually. One center line looks right, one does not. This one looks right to me, so I'm done:

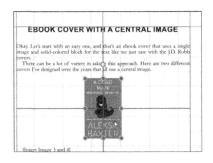

All I need to do now is delete the text that told me to insert my image. (We're ignoring for the moment the fact that I was supposed to insert two images here on this line. If I'd actually done that I would have had to insert both images, group them, and then center the group.)

Okay. I will also often format the next paragraph to remove the indent. Whether you do or not is a style preference, just be consistent throughout that title whichever choice you make.

So I inserted my first image and it's now time to insert the next one, but we have an issue. Look here:

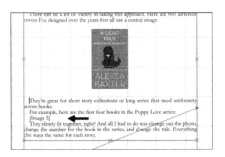

There is no way that image five, whatever it is, will fit at the bottom of this page. Not happening. But because we're using picture frames for this Affinity isn't going to automatically adjust my text placement for me either.

I need to tell Affinity to move all of the text below "Puppy Love series:" to the next page. I do this by inserting a Frame Break using Text->Insert->Breaks->Frame Break right after that colon.

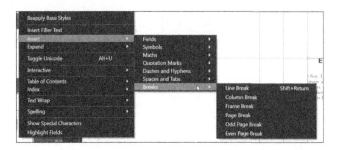

A frame break pushes all of the text below that point to the next text frame, which in this case is also on the next page.

It also seems to insert an actual line as well. So if that happens to you, just delete it.

Now I can place my image at the top of the next page and have all of the text that should be after that image where it belongs.

With that problem solved, it's the same process again for this image. Add my picture frame. Put my image in the picture frame. Resize the image. Resize the frame to match. Move the image so they're overlapped. Move the picture frame into position. Delete the note. Done.

Now I want to walk you through how to change that import setting for the picture frame so that the image comes right into the frame.

First step is to add the picture frame. That changes the dynamic menu up top to the one for the picture frame and gives us a Properties option.

Clicking on Properties gives me a series of choices about how I bring in an image into my frame.

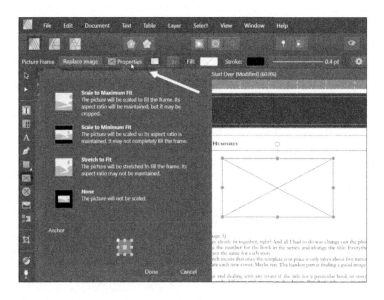

Right now it's set to just anchor in the top left corner of the page. (You can see that the little box in the anchor section that's in the top left-corner is a bright white compared to the others which are gray.)

Interestingly enough, once I fixed this appearance I couldn't replicate it, so it could've been some weird bug I triggered where there was no option selected up top, but I'm just going to continue as if that's a possible option.

To get the picture to come into the picture frame directly you need to choose one of the four options above that.

For what we're doing here, we do NOT want to use Stretch To Fit because it will skew the image by stretching it to the height and width of the picture frame.

Scale To Maximum Fit will try to fit the image to either the width or height of the frame, whichever creates the maximum fit. This means part of the image will fall outside of the frame.

Here that is. See how it came in inside the picture frame and matched the height of the frame but the image is wider than you can see here?

If we use this option, that means we need to be much more careful about the DPI because I don't know what DPI this image is now. I told Affinity to worry about putting the image in the frame, not to worry about the DPI.

Let's go to the Resource Manager to see:

And, yep, see, that's a problem. We need a DPI of 300 or more, but because I asked Affinity to scale to my randomly-drawn picture frame, the image came in at 260 DPI.

Even if this image looked like it was the size I want, it would need to be smaller to get that DPI over 300.

Scale To Minimum Fit tries to fit the image into the frame entirely which means that there will likely be space around the top, bottom, or edge but the image will be fully visible. So in this example the image would have a lot of space probably on the top.

It also is going to have similar issues with DPI. We won't know until we check what the image DPI is.

The final option there, None, does not try to fit the image to the picture frame. It simply brings the image into the frame. And, from what I can tell, does so at the DPI set in your document. That's the one I like for this purpose.

(I should add that I found it better to set my document DPI to 305 instead of 300 because every so often an imported image showed in the Resource Manager with a DPI of 299 after it imported.)

* * *

Now let me show you how to bring in an image without using a picture frame.

First, click where the image should go. Next, go straight to the Place Image Tool, click on it and select your image. The image should come in as-is on top of your text:

(See the text peeking out along the edges of that image there?)

When an image imports like this, the image is "anchored" to where you clicked when you inserted it:

It's a little hard to see, but there's a blue line connecting that image to the spot I clicked when I inserted the image and there's a blue dot at that location to mark the spot.

I tell Affinity to jump the image just like we did with the picture frame, and I get this:

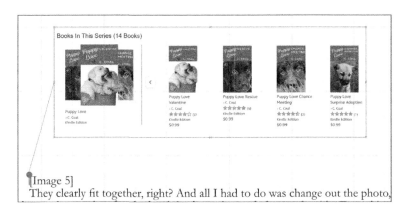

You can better see the anchor now, right? But the text is no longer behind the image like it was before.

Now. The main differences between this approach and the one I showed you with picture frames is that the image will move with the text.

So here I inserted a page and half worth of enters to move the text to the next page, and the image went with that text:

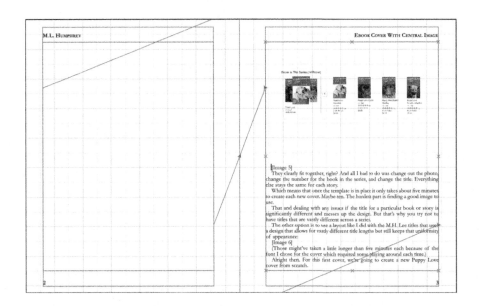

Had I done the same thing with this image in a picture frame, the picture frame would not have moved at all. It would still be in that top left corner of the prior page, regardless of where the text it belonged with went.

So directly inserting an image ensures that the image will stay with its text.

But you have to be careful what text you anchor the image to. I just deleted that text about image 5 and it took the image with it. Always anchor to the text above or below where you want to insert your image. Sometimes the text above will be the better choice, sometimes the text below. (At least in my experience when I was still trying to work with pinned images.)

To work with positioning the image, you need to use the Pinning studio. I don't keep that open, but here it is:

There are two types of images, floating and inline.

You're generally going to want a floating image. Inline images appear to be more for, say, a drop cap. Affinity's help text says that inline images are treated like a character within the text.

The image I pinned above was a floating image. In the Float tab, the Horizontal Align setting will let you align the image to the left, center, or right of the text frame or page. You want Inside Center for Frame to center in the text fame.

Vertical Align will change the vertical positioning of the image relative to the pin.

The horizontal and vertical offset values are where you can specify the exact position of the image relative to where it's pinned.

To unpin an image, click on unpin. That will let you manually move the image around.

To repin the image just click on Float or Inline in the Pinning dialogue box.

You can left-click and drag a pin in your text to anchor the image to different text.

Affinity's help instructions actually have you insert the image first and then pin it. To do that, don't click anywhere in the text first, just place the image and then click on the image and use the Pinning studio to pin it.

You can also pin an image using the menu option at the top that appears when you have an image selected as shown here:

For full position control, though, you need the pinning studio open.

To place a border around an image like this, change the settings for Stroke while the image is selected. Here, for example, I've placed a dark black border around the image:

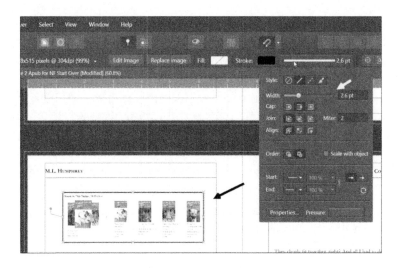

After walking through this here, I have less problem with using pinned images, but I know that I did run into issues properly centering my pinned images when I tried to work with them before. It could've been because of indented paragraphs of text (which can be an issue in Word), but whatever it was I just moved on to picture frames instead of try to get it working consistently.

But pinned images definitely do have the advantage of staying with your text no matter what, so if that's really important for you and your process, absolutely use pinned images instead of picture frames to place your images.

Okay. Next let's talk about image adjustments.

IMAGE ADJUSTMENTS

To wrap this up I want to talk about one final topic and that's making adjustments to your images. This may have something to do with my document and image settings, but I found with the first book that I published using Affinity that my images didn't work well. My paler images were too pale and my darker images were too dark.

Keep in mind that when you set Affinity to grayscale that means the program is converting that image for you behind the scenes. And it seems to me that the way it converts images to grayscale by default may be different from how Word does it, because I never felt the need to make these sorts of adjustments when dealing with images in Word.

I say all of that to basically tell you that you'll need to decide for yourself if your images need adjusting or not. It's quite possible they don't because of your settings or the images you're using. Or you may just be much fancier than me and manually adjust every image to grayscale yourself to make it perfect, which I know some people do.

What I've ended up doing with my Affinity files is take my paler images and darken them and take my darker images and make them lighter. Which means in print some of the images we're about to look at may not look all that great because I want you to see the difference and the adjustments I make.

The top image here is from the fiction layouts Affinity guide without adjustment. The bottom one is that same image with a brightness adjustment applied:

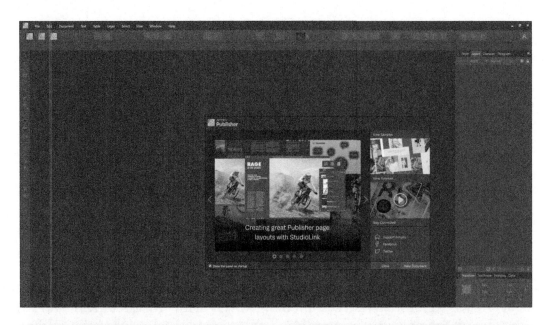

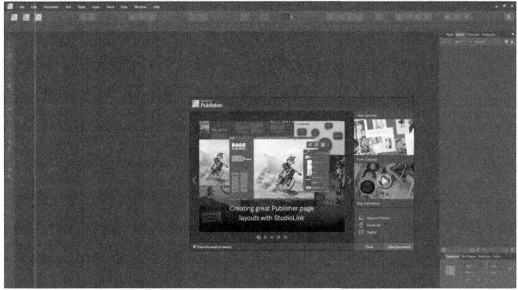

For the ebook version I've done a screenshot of the two to hopefully show the difference.

See how the top image is darker and perhaps a little harder to read or distinguish different components?

Here is an adjustment for an image that's mostly pale lines with the top being the original and the bottom being the adjusted image:

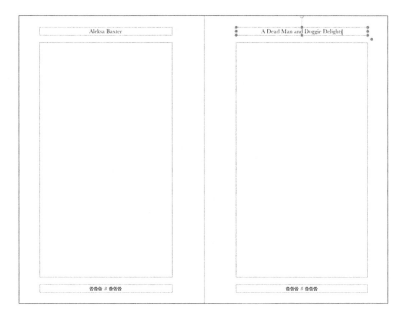

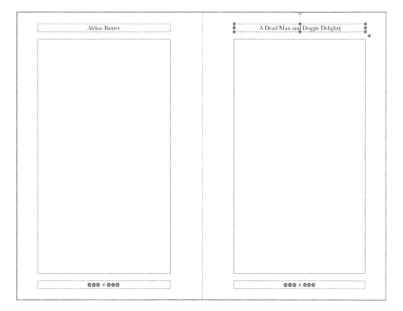

Whether your images will need this sort of adjustment or not is your call. All I can do is tell you to print your document or order a proof copy of your book to see what the images actually look like in print on the page to decide.

If you do decide an adjustments is needed, I use the Brightness and Contrast adjustments option that can be found at the bottom of the studios section:

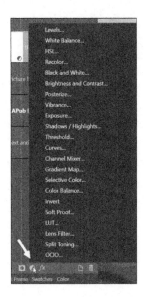

You can also get there through Layer->New Adjustment in the top menu.

For each of the above I only changed the Brightness level. For the dark images, I used a positive value of about 35% and for the light images I used a negative value of about -25%.

But again, you'll need to find what works for you and your images. For example, I just tried a negative 50% adjustment on that second image and it certainly made those lines much darker, but I'd have to print it to see how the text renders when I do that.

Once you add an adjustment to an image it will show below that image in your Layers studio as a white box with the name of the type of adjustment listed:

You can toggle that adjustment on and off using the checkbox for that adjustment layer.

You can also delete that layer if you want to permanently remove the adjustment. (I sometimes find it easier to remove an adjustment and re-add it rather than try to adjust from where it already is.)

In order to delete just the adjustment layer and not the image as well, be sure to click on the white square for that layer. If you click elsewhere it tends to have a habit of selecting the image layer as well.

Okay, so that's my very basic image adjustment guidance. A true graphic design pro could give you far more guidance on this than I have, but that at least should help you get started with image adjustments.

EXPORT AS PDF

One more topic before we wrap up. We touched on this in prior books, but I want to cover it again, because there's something you need to adjust for if you have a lot of images in your document.

IngramSpark says that they want a PDF/X-1a:2003 file and for fiction layouts that were just using one simple little image that was fine to use in the Affinity export to PDF step. But I found that it didn't work for my books because the images, even if my document was set to be grayscale, exported as color images. Which meant I was leaving the conversion from color to grayscale up to IngramSpark or Amazon.

Not something I was sure I wanted to do. I did with my original Excel books and that worked fine, but why go through the effort of choosing Grayscale in Affinity only to not use it, right?

So what I did was start with that setting in the dropdown and then click on the More option in the dialogue box:

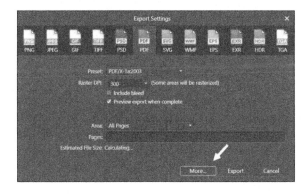

That opened an additional dialogue box:

The box I need to have checked is "Convert Image Color Spaces." As you can see here, it's grayed out. I also don't want it to compress JPG images even though I use TIFF images. And you don't want to embed the ICC profile either since that can generate an error message on IngramSpark.

So this is what I end up with:

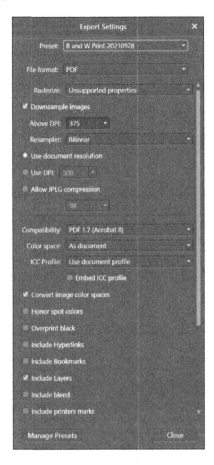

The first step to get this to all work is to change that Compatibility dropdown to PDF 1.7 which allows for conversion of the image color spaces and makes those checkboxes become available for edit.

I won't promise you that these are the best settings, because I can't. All I can tell you is that if you're reading this in print that they're the settings I used for the book that's in your hands.

Also, note that because I don't want to think about this every single time I export a print book with images in it, that I made it into a preset that's available in my dropdown menu. I did that with the Manage Presets option at the bottom of that larger settings menu.

CONCLUSION

Alright. I think that pretty much covers what I do in Affinity Publisher that's either a more-advanced fiction skill or that's specific to non-fiction. And across this four-book series we've definitely at least touched upon all of the tools and ways in which I use the program.

But as much as I do with Affinity Publisher, I do not have all of the answers. The key when you get stuck is to go find the people who do, which is why I love their forums and product help, because I think they're both very nice to people and provide a lot of solid information.

First, as I mentioned in the first book of this series, the folks at Affinity have excellent instructional videos available on their website: https://affinity.serif.com/en-us/learn/

I watched them all when I was starting out because I didn't know what I didn't know.

The folks at Affinity also have huge, massive, beautiful books they publish on each program that are available through their website and on Amazon and probably every other major retailer.

I am cheap and very bad at following something like that, so I've never bought them, but if their books are the same quality as their product and their videos, then I'd say those are probably worth considering as a resource on your shelf, but I suspect the focus is going to be far different from the focus in these books which was specifically on self-publishing.

I'd expect they're also far more geared towards design professionals who already have that solid graphic design background, but I could be wrong. So maybe check those out.

Also, I use their Affinity Publisher help wiki on a regular basis: https://affinity.help/publisher/en-US.lproj/index.html

Probably not as often as I should. Many of the discoveries I had while writing this book were from there. I'd start to say something here and then think, "Is that really true?" and go find the answer.

Usually their help wiki comes up when I do an internet search for "Affinity Publisher X" where X is what I'm trying to figure out. But you can also navigate through it using the menu options on the side.

And then, last but certainly not least, there are the user forums: https:// forum.affinity.serif.com/

That trick I shared here about putting text in a text frame and hiding it behind the book cover to feed your table of contents came from a post there that I happened to see when I was looking for something else.

The forums are another one I've never gone to directly, but have instead found through an internet search. Just keep in mind that from what I can tell this is a product that they've been constantly improving since its original release, so sometimes I'll find an answer from 2018 where someone says you can't do something but it turns out you can now.

So if you see a "that's not an option" answer and it's from more than about six months ago, keep digging to be sure.

And you can always message me, of course. mlhumphreywriter@gmail.com. I'm pretty good at finding answers to things I don't know and then testing them out and gaining an understanding of them.

So even if I don't know the answer when you email me, I'm very likely to go dig it up for you. Just don't abuse that privilege. (I had someone on the Excel side who seemed to think I provide free consulting services for their company who I finally had to cut off.)

Finally, if you want to see the topics that were covered in this book "live", there is a video course version of this book available at https://ml-humphrey.teachable.com/courses. Use code MLH50 to get fifty percent off.

Anyway. I really do like the Affinity suite of products. And I think they really have helped me take things to the next level. I hope the same is true for you.

Good luck with it. And reach out if you get stuck.

APPENDIX A: QUICK TAKES

AUTHOR NAME

FIELD EDIT

Fields studio. Click on field next to Author. Type author name. Enter.

INSERT

Artistic Text Tool. Click on location in document where field should be inserted. Go to Fields studio. Double-click on Author.

BOOK TITLE

FIELD EDIT

Fields studio. Click on field next to Title. Type book title. Enter.

INSERT

Artistic Text Tool. Click on location in document where field should be inserted. Go to Fields studio. Double-click on Title.

CHAPTER TITLE

INSERT AS HEADER

Click on location in document. Go to top menu. Text. Insert Fields. Section Name. Where the chapter title was assigned as the section name.

COLUMNS

BALANCE TEXT

Click on the text frame. Go to the Columns section of the Text Frame studio and click the "Balance Text Columns" box.

CHANGE NUMBER

Click on text frame. Go to dynamic menu up top and change value for Columns.

DIVIDING LINE

Click on the text frame. Open the Text Frame studio and go to the Column Rules section and change the Stroke settings. Top and Bottom values will determine whether the text fills the entire space. Start and End dropdowns can be used to put a shape at the end of the divider line, like an arrow.

FORMAT

Click on the text frame. Open the Text Frame studio and go to the Columns section.

GAP BETWEEN

Click on text frame. Go to dynamic menu up top and change the number in the field to the right of the number of columns setting. Or open the Text Frame studio and go to the Columns section and adjust the value for the gutter there.

EXPORT

PDF

To export a PDF of your document, go to File, Export, and choose the PDF option. For review purposes, All Spreads is better because it will keep facing pages together in the PDF. For KDP and IngramSpark upload, use All Pages.

IMAGE

ADJUSTMENTS

To adjust an image, go to Layer->New Adjustment and choose the type of image adjustment you need. You can also use the Adjustments option at the bottom of the Layers studio to see the list of available adjustments.

CENTER

Left-click and drag the image until you see the green center line. For a standard book, be sure to drag from the outer edge of the page because there will be two center lines, one for the entire page and one for the text frame. For a pinned image, use the Pinning studio.

DPI

The image DPI will increase as your image size decreases.

FLOAT

To float an image, open the Pinning studio and click on the Float tab.

IMPORT PREFERENCES WITH PICTURE FRAME

When importing an image into a picture frame, you can set how the image imports using the Preferences option in the dynamic menu after you click on the picture frame.

INLINE

To make an image an inline image, open the Pinning studio and click on the Inline tab.

INSERT

Place Image Tool. Select image to insert. Open. Image may automatically insert. If not, click and drag in workspace until desired size.

INSERT IN PICTURE FRAME

Click on picture frame layer. Place Image Tool. Select image to insert. Open. Your import preferences will determine if the image comes in at the document DPI or at a size that best fits the picture frame.

MOVE

Move Tool. Click on image layer or directly on image if not in a picture frame. Click on image, hold left-click and drag to desired location. Use snapping to align along edges or center.

MOVE PIN

For a pinned image, you can left-click and drag on the pin to move what text the image is pinned to.

PIN TO TEXT

If you click into your text before inserting an image, the image will be pinned to your text when it inserts. If an image is not pinned to text, you can use the Pinning studio or the pin option in the dynamic menu up top to pin the image to your text after the fact.

QUALITY

For print files, use a DPI of at least 300 for grayscale images and 600 for black and white line drawings. Go to File->Document Setup to specify your document DPI. Set it slightly above the desired DPI if importing images.

REPLACE

Document top menu option. Resource Manager. Select image. Replace. Select new image. Open. Close resource manager. Or, with Move Tool selected, click on image and use Replace Image option in dynamic menu.

RESIZE

Move Tool. Click on image layer or directly on image if not in a picture frame. Option A: Transform studio. Lock Aspect Ratio. Change height or width value. Option B: Click on blue circle in corner and drag at an angle to resize proportionately. Or click on blue circle along any edge to change height or width only. This will skew most images.

UNPIN

Layers studio. Click on image layer. Open Pinning studio. Click on Unpin.

INDEX

INSERT

Click intro document where you want to place the index. Go to the Index studio. Click on the Insert Index option. Or go to the top menu, Text, Index, Insert Index.

MANUAL EDITS

Once inserted, an index can be manually edited but those edits will be overwritten if the index is ever updated.

TEXT STYLE

The index entries use text styles so text can be edited and then the text style updated to apply that change to all entries.

UPDATE

Either go to the top menu and then Text, Index, and Update Index. Or use the Index studio and choose the Update option at the top. If the index does not update, delete the existing text of the index, and insert a new index instead.

INDEX MARKERS AND TOPICS

CROSS-REFERENCE

Both topics need to already exist. Right-click on the topic you want to cross-reference from and choose Add Cross Reference. In the Add Cross-Reference dialogue box select the topic you want to reference to in the dropdown menu.

INSERT

Select the text you want to use as your index text or click into the text where you want the marker. Either go to the Index studio and click on the Insert Marker option at the top or go to the top menu, Text, Index, Insert Index Mark.

MOVE ENTRY LEVEL

Go to the Index studio and left-click on the topic name you want to move. Drag it to the topic you want to place it under. Or, right-click on the topic name choose to Edit Topic, and change the Parent Topic information to either add or remove a parent level.

NAME (ASSIGN)

In the Insert Index Mark dialogue box, type the name into the Topic Name field.

NAME (EDIT)

Click once on the name. Click again to select the text. Type in your new name. Or right-click, Edit Topic, and change the value in the Topic Name field.

PARENT TOPIC (ASSIGN)

The parent topic you want to use needs to be in the index already. When you open the Insert Index Mark dialogue box or the Edit Index Mark dialogue box, choose the parent topic you want from the Parent Topic dropdown menu.

PARENT TOPIC (REMOVE PAGE NUMBERING)

Remove any underlying citations from the Parent Topic in the Index studio. Either move them to the subtopic or delete them using the trash can icon.

MASTER PAGE

ADD NEW

Pages studio. Master Pages section. Right-click on existing master page. Option A: Choose Insert Master. Click OK to create a new master page that has the basic properties of the existing master page. Option B: Choose Duplicate to create an exact duplicate of the existing master page.

MOVE

Pages studio. Master Pages section. Click on master page and drag. Blue line along edge will show where master page will move to. Release left-click when where wanted.

RENAME

Pages studio. Master pages section. Click on master page thumbnail. Click on name of master page. Type in new name. Enter.

MERGE DOCUMENTS

ADD DOCUMENT

Go to the page of the existing document in the Pages studio where you want to add the document, right-click, and choose Add Pages from the dropdown. Navigate to and select the document to import. In the Add Pages dialogue box choose All Pages, After, Pages, and verify that it shows the page number for that page. OK.

PRE-IMPORT SET-UP

If your documents are set to have a right-hand page start, be sure that the document you're importing into has only one page on the left-hand side at the end in order to maintain pages on the correct side of the page.

NEW DOCUMENT PRESET

RENAME

Right-click on thumbnail for preset. Rename Preset. Type new name. OK.

PAGE NUMBER

CHANGE NUMBERING STYLE

Pages studio. Pages section. Right-click on page and choose Edit Section. Click on section name that contains the pages where you want to change the numbering style. Choose the new style from the Number Style dropdown menu. Close.

INSERT

Master page. Artistic Text Tool. Click where you want page number placed. Text top menu choice. Insert. Fields. Page Number.

RESTART AT 1

Pages studio. Pages section. Click on page where you want to restart at 1. Right-click. Start New Section. (Or Edit Section if one has already been started.) Click button for Restart Page Numbering At. Enter 1. Confirm numbering style is correct. If not, choose the correct one from the dropdown menu.

PAGES

ADD PAGES

Pages studio. Pages section. Right-click on an existing page or page spread. Add Pages. Choose the number of pages, whether to insert before or after, the page number (based on left-hand panel numbering where the pages should be inserted), and select the master page to use for the inserted pages. OK.

APPLY MASTER PAGE

Pages studio. Pages section. Right-click on the pages where you want to apply the master page. (Be sure that both pages are selected in a two-page spread.) Apply Master. Choose desired master page from dropdown menu. OK.

DELETE PAGES

Pages studio. Pages section. Click on page or page spread that you want to delete. Right-click. Delete X Pages. If there is more than one page spread that you want to delete, click on page spread at one end of the page range, hold down the shift key and click on the page spread at the other end of the page range. Right-click. Delete X Pages.

PICTURE FRAME

BORDER

Click on the Picture Frame. Go to the dynamic menu up top and change the line width next to the Stroke option.

INSERT

Picture Frame Rectangle Tool. Click and drag to create frame on canvas.

JUMP

To have text jump an inserted picture frame, click on the Picture Frame and then use the Show Text Wrap Settings in the top menu and choose Jump for the Wrap Style.

RESIZE TO IMAGE

Click on Picture Frame and in dynamic menu choose the Size Frame to Content option.

WRAP TEXT AROUND

To have text wrap around an inserted picture frame, click on the Picture Frame and then use the Show Text Wrap Settings in the top menu and choose Square or Tight for the Wrap Style.

RECOVER FILE

RECOVER FILE

If Affinity ever crashes and closes while you were working on a file, reopen the program and try to reopen the file. Affinity should tell you that there is a recovery version of the file available. Choose to open the recovery version and then check for the last edits you made to determine if any of your work was lost and needs to be redone.

SECTION

ASSIGN NAME

Pages studio. Pages section. Right-click and Edit Section. In Section Manager, click on the section that you want to rename. Type name into Section Name field. Close.

CHANGE START PAGE

Pages studio. Pages section. Right-click and Edit Section. In Section Manager, change the "Start On Page".

CONTINUE PAGE NUMBERING

Pages studio. Pages section. Right-click and Edit Section. For the section that needs to continue page numbering, check the box to continue page numbering.

CREATE

Pages studio. Pages section. Right-click on the page that you want to have start the new section, Start New Section. In Section Manager, assign name if desired and verify page numbering format and whether it should restart or continue.

EDIT

Pages studio. Pages section. Right-click and Edit Section.

DELETE

Pages studio. Pages section. Right-click and Edit Section. In Section Manager, click on the section you want to delete and use the small trash can icon to delete it.

INSERT NAME

Click on location in header where field should be inserted. Go to Text top menu option. Insert. Fields. Section Name.

RESTART PAGE NUMBERING

Pages studio. Pages section. Right-click and Edit Section. For the section that needs to restart page numbering, check the box to "restart page numbering at", verify the page number, generally 1, and the number style.

SNAPPING

ENABLE

Go to the horseshoe shaped magnet image in the top center. Click on the dropdown arrow. Check the box next to Enable Snapping.

STUDIO

MOVE OR ANCHOR

Left-click on studio tab and drag to desired location. To anchor, either drag until you see a blue box appear and then release or drag to where other studios are already anchored and add to those tabs.

STUDIO PRESET

ADD NEW

Arrange studios as desired. View top menu option. Studio Presets. Add Preset. Type name. OK.

APPLY

View top menu option. Studio Presets. Select desired preset. Or Ctrl + Shift + [Number].

DELETE

View top menu option. Studio Presets. Manage Studio Presets. Select preset name. Delete. Close.

RENAME

View top menu option. Studio Presets. Manage Studio Presets. Select preset name. Rename. Type in new name. OK. Close.

SAVE CHANGES

Make desired changes to studio preset arrangement. View top menu option. Studio Presets. Add Preset. Type in exact same name as before. OK. Agree to overwrite old preset.

TABLE OF CONTENTS

ENTRIES (INDENT)

Click onto a sample of the text you want to indent in the Table of Contents. Go to the Paragraph studio and set a left indent to the value you want. Update the text style when done.

ENTRIES (SELECT)

Assign one or more unique text styles to each text entry in the document that you want included in the table of contents. Go to the Table of Contents studio and under Style Name, check the check box for each text style you want to include.

ENTRIES (UPDATE)
You can manually update any text in the table of contents, but it is better to update the text in the document and then refresh your table of contents.

ENTRIES (WHEN NO TEXT AVAILABLE FOR SELECTION)
If you ever have a situation where you need a table of contents entry but there is no visible text to use for it, you can create a text frame, place that text you need into the frame, and then hide the frame on the page you need the table of contents entry to start on.

FOR SECTION
To insert a table of contents that covers only a section of a book, insert the table of contents like normal but be sure to check the box for "Stop at Next TOC" and to use different text styles than the ones used in the overarching table of contents.

INSERT
Click into the document where you want your table of contents inserted. Option one, go to the Table of Contents studio, click on the Insert option on the left at the top. Option two, top menu, Text, Table of Contents, Insert Table of Contents.

OVERARCHING
For a table of contents that covers the entire document when other tables of contents exist in the document, be sure to use specific text styles for just that table of contents and to NOT check the "Stop at Next TOC" option.

PAGE NUMBERS
To include page numbers, right-click on the preferences dropdown for that text style and check the box for "Include Page Number." To remove page numbers, uncheck it.

SEPARATORS BETWEEN TEXT AND PAGE NUMBER
Go to the Separator section of the Table of Contents studio. Use the dropdown menu to select your desired separator or type into the field. For a

dotted line, right-click on the text style and choose to edit it. Go to the Tab Stops section and choose the Tab Stop Leader Character option that has a period in the parens.

UPDATE

Go to the Table of Contents studio and click on the Update option at the top. If you have multiple tables of contents in your document, be sure the TOC dropdown shows the table of contents you want to update or choose to update all. Or go to Text, Table of Contents, Update Table of Contents or click on Fix in the Preflight studio.

TEXT

ADD SPACE BETWEEN LINES

Artistic Text Tool. Select paragraph of text. Paragraph studio. Spacing section. Leading dropdown. Choose desired option. Or for multiple lines of the same style, click on Space Between Same Styles and set a value.

ADD SPECIAL SYMBOLS OR CHARACTERS

Artistic Text Tool. Click into workspace where desired. Go to View top menu. Studio. Glyph Browser. Or if docked, open glyph browser. Find desired symbol or character. Double-click on symbol or character to insert.

ALIGNMENT

Artistic Text Tool. Click on the paragraph or paragraphs. Menu choices above workspace. Four images with lines. Align Left, Align Center, Align Right, or dropdown menu for Justify Left, Justify Center, Justify Right, Justify All, Align Towards Spine, Align Away From Spine. Or, to the right of that, dropdown menu for Top Align, Center Vertically, Bottom Align, Justify Vertically. The horizontal alignment options are also available at the top of the Paragraph studio.

ALL CAPS OR SMALL CAPS

Artistic Text Tool. Select the text to be formatted. Go to Character studio. Typography section. Click on the two capital Ts (TT) to apply all caps. Click on the capital T with a smaller capital T (TT) to apply small caps. Check your text entries for issues with using a capital letter or lower case letter when working with small caps because the two do look different in small caps.

APPLY HYPHENATION

Artistic Text Tool. Select text. Paragraph studio. Hyphenation section. Click on box next to Use Auto-Hyphenation. Change values as needed.

APPLY TRACKING

Artistic Text Tool. Select text. Character studio. Positioning and Transform section. Second option in the left-hand column, Tracking. Click arrow for dropdown menu. Choose desired change.

BOLD

Artistic Text Tool. Select text. Ctrl + B. Or click on B in top menu. Or go to Character studio and choose the Strong option from the Style dropdown menu at the top. Only works if there is a bold version of the font available.

FONT

Artistic Text Tool. Select text. Top menu, left-hand side. Font dropdown. Choose font. Or select text and go to Character studio font dropdown at top.

INDENT PARAGRAPH

Artistic Text Tool. Select paragraph. Paragraph studio. Spacing section. Second option on left-hand side. (First Line Indent). Add value.

ITALICS

Artistic Text Tool. Select text. Ctrl + I. Or click on I in top menu. Or go to Character studio and choose the Emphasis option from the Style dropdown menu at the top. Only works if there is an italic version of the font available.

JUMP IMAGE

Move Tool. Select image. Click on Show Text Wrap Settings option in top menu. In Text Wrap dialogue box choose Jump as desired Wrap Style.

KEEP TOGETHER

Artistic Text Tool. Select second paragraph or line that you want to keep together. Go to the Paragraph studio. Flow Options section. Check box for Keep With Previous Paragraph.

LINE SPACING (LEADING)

Artistic Text Tool. Select paragraph. Paragraph studio. Spacing section. Change value in Leading dropdown. Default is usually a good place to start.

MOVE TO NEXT PAGE

Click right after the text that's before the text you want to move to the next page. Go to Text->Insert->Break->Frame Break to move the text to the next frame.

ORPHANS REMOVE AUTOMATICALLY

Artistic Text Tool. Select text. Paragraph studio. Flow Options. Check box for Prevent Orphaned First Lines.

SIZE

Artistic Text Tool. Select text. Top menu, left-hand side. Font size dropdown. Choose size or type in size. Or select text and go to Character studio font size dropdown at top.

SMALL CAPS

See *All Caps or Small Caps*.

UNDERLINE

Artistic Text Tool. Select text. Ctrl + U. Or click on the underlined U in top menu. Or go to Character studio and choose one of the underlined U options from the Decorations section.

WEIGHT

Artistic Text Tool. Select text. Top menu, left-hand side. Font weight dropdown. Choose from available weights for that font. Or select text and go to Character studio font weight dropdown at top.

WIDOWS REMOVE AUTOMATICALLY

Artistic Text Tool. Select text. Paragraph studio. Flow Options. Check box for Prevent Widowed Last Lines.

WRAP AROUND IMAGE

Move Tool. Select image. Click on Show Text Wrap Settings option in top menu. In Text Wrap dialogue box choose Wrap Style.

TEXT FLOW

AUTO FLOW

Pages studio. Pages section. Double-click on last page spread in section. Go to right-hand edge of last text frame in workspace. Click on red circle to see red arrow. Hold down shift key and click on red arrow. Affinity will flow the text to as many page spreads as needed using the same master page spread format.

FROM ONE TEXT FRAME TO ANOTHER ADD

Click on blue arrow along the edge of the first text frame. Click on second text frame.

FROM ONE TEXT FRAME TO ANOTHER REMOVE

Click on the blue arrow along the edge of the first text frame. Click back onto the first text frame.

TEXT FRAME

ALIGN OR POSITION

Frame Text Tool or Move Tool. Left-click on text frame and hold as you drag. Look for red and green alignment lines to center or align to other elements in workspace. (Turn on Snapping if there are no red or green lines.)

INSERT

Frame Text Tool on left-hand side. Click and drag in workspace.

TEXT STYLE

APPLY

Artistic Text Tool. Select text. Use dropdown menu at top to apply style. Or go to Text Styles studio and click on desired style. Or use shortcut if one is associated with the style.

BASED ON OTHER STYLE

To base a text style off of another style, first apply the existing text style. Next, make any edits to create the new style. And then save as new style.

IMPORTED

If you use the import text style option or are merging two files and it appears, you can choose which text styles to import using the checkbox on the far left. If this is for an import with overlapping text style names click on the Rename To option to bring in the text style but with a new name, click on OK to bring it in with the same name, or choose which of the two styles to keep if there is a conflict identified.

KEYBOARD SHORTCUT

For a new style, add keyboard shortcut in the Style section of the Create Paragraph Style dialogue box where it says Keyboard Shortcut. (Don't type the description, just use the shortcut when you're clicked into the box.) For an existing style, go to the Text Styles studio, right-click on the style name, Edit [Style Name], and then in the Style section of the Edit Text Style dialogue box, add the keyboard shortcut.

NEW

Artistic Text Tool. Select text. Format text. Text style dropdown in top menu. New Style. Give style a name and keyboard shortcut if desired. OK.

UPDATE OR CHANGE

Artistic Text Tool. Select text with style to be updated. Make edits. Click on paragraph symbol with a swish that's to the right of the text style dropdown menu in the top menu area. Or, go to Text Styles studio, right-click on text style name, Edit [Style Name], make edits in Edit Text Style dialogue box, OK.

APPENDIX B: CREATE A BOOK
FROM AN EXISTING FILE

1. Delete out any old text from the main body of the existing file and delete all pages except the front matter, first chapter start page, and the first Text and Text page.

2. If you want to use different fonts in your document than are used in the existing file, change the fonts for the relevant text styles. If your document is set up with primary and secondary text styles then you only need to change the primary text style for each font.

3. Replace the image(s) in the document or delete the images from the master pages, if needed.

4. After you've replaced any image, make sure it is still positioned properly on each master page.

5. Edit the text on the Title page to reflect the correct book title.

6. Edit the text on the Also By page to reflect the correct author name, series name, and title name.

7. Edit the text on the Copyright page to show the copyright year, copyright name, and ISBN for the title.

8. Go to the Fields studio and edit the Author and Title fields to show the correct author name and book title.

9. Paste in the main body text of your document.

10. If your text imported with an assigned style or styles, you can use find and replace to change the assigned styles to the ones you need. Otherwise, apply the main body text style for now.

11. Flow your text by Shift + clicking on the red arrow on the right-hand edge of the right-hand text box of the last page which should be a Text and Text page.

12. Assign chapter header and paragraph text styles to the first page of the main body of the book. Double-check that the document looks good. That all images are placed properly, chapter starts are where you want them, paragraphs are formatted as desired, etc. If not, fix those issues in your master pages or text styles before proceeding.

13. Walk through your main body text and assign chapter header, first paragraph, and section break formatting to the text as needed. Also change the master page assigned for each spread when needed. And fix any widows, orphans, one-line chapter ends, etc.

14. At the end of the document you may need to either reflow the text again to cover all of your text and/or there may be extra pages that weren't used that need to be deleted.

15. Add your back matter. At a minimum this should include an About the Author page.

16. Export to PDF (PDF X-1a:2003 should work for most purposes) being sure to change the Area selection to All Pages from All Spreads.

17. Review the PDF file and verify that all pages exported and look as expected. Specifically check headers, footers, paragraph formatting, master page assignment, chapter header and section break formatting, front matter, and back matter. Also check for single-line chapter endings, widows, orphans, short words at the end of paragraphs, and too much white space in justified paragraphs.

18. For any issues, fix them in the Affinity file and then re-export and re-review. When final, the PDF should be ready to upload for printing.

INDEX

A

Affinity Help 259

Affinity Website 5

Author Name 261

    Field Edit 261

    Insert 63, 261

B

Back Matter 131, 137

Bleed 17

Book Title 261

    Field Edit 261

    Insert 66, 261

C

Chapter Title 261

    Insert as Header 178–179, 261

Color Layout 17

Columns 261

    Balance Text 190, 261

    Change Number 185–186, 261

    Dividing Line 188–189, 261

    Format 187, 262

    Gap Between 186, 262

Cover Design Course 6

Cover Mockups 6

D

DPI 17

E

Export 262

    PDF 216, 255–257, 262

Export a PDF 141–143

F

Fields Studio 63

Find and Replace

    Chapter Headings 99

    Flaw 124

    Paragraph Style 98

Section Breaks 97

Find and Replace Studio 98

Font Bundles 7

Font Choice 54

Formatting for Print 3, 54–55, 57, 93, 110, 113, 116, 143

Front Matter 67–68

G

Glyph Browser Studio 55

I

Image 262

    Adjustments 249–253, 262

    Align 33, 46

    Border 247

    Center 46, 262

    Change 41–42

    Delete 66

    DPI 235, 238, 243, 262

    Embedded 17

    Float 245, 247, 262

    Import Preferences 242–244, 263

    In Own Layer 30

    Inline 247, 263

    Insert 29, 31–32, 244, 263

    Insert in Picture Frame 237–238, 263

    Linked 17

    Lock Aspect Ratio 33

    Move 32, 45, 263

    Move Pin 263

    Pin to Text 245–247, 263

    Quality 234, 263

    Replace 41–42, 264

    Resize 45, 239, 264

    Unpin 30, 247, 264

Index 264

    Insert 193, 198, 264

    Manual Edits 204, 264

    Text Style 264

    Update 198, 264

Index Markers and Topics 264

    Cross-Reference 203, 264

    Insert 196–197, 203, 265

    Move Entry Level 201–202, 265

    Name (Assign) 265

    Name (Edit) 265

    Parent Topic (Assign) 199–200, 202, 265

    Parent Topic (Remove Page Numbering) 200, 265

    Rename 203

L

Large Print 18, 95

M

Main Body Text 75

Margins 17

Master Page 265

    Add New 265

    Changes To 51

    Definition 21

    Duplicate 44

    Move 54, 266

    Rename 22, 44, 266

Master Page Examples

    Also By Page 43–48, 58

    Chapter Start and Text 119–120

    Copyright and Chapter Start 53–55

    No Text and Chapter Start 117–118

    No Text and Section Start 135

    Simple Title Page 25–31

    Text and Chapter Start 61–64

    Text and No Text 133

    Text and Text 65–66

Merge Documents 266

    Add Document 214–215, 220, 222, 266

    Pre-Import Set-Up 212–213, 220, 266

N

New Document 15–19

New Document Preset 266

    Rename 18, 266

P

Page Number 266

    Change Numbering Style 266

    Insert 58, 267

    Restart at 1 125–127, 267

Pages 267

    Add New Section 126

    Add Pages 35, 49–50, 267

    Apply Master Page 105–108, 267

    Changes To 51

    Delete Pages 76, 129–130, 267

Pages Studio 22

Picture Frame 267

    Border 267

    Insert 236, 267

    Jump 236, 268

    Move 240

    Resize to Image 240, 268

    Wrap Text Around 237, 268

Preflight Studio 33, 139–140

Preview Document 39

R

Recover File 221, 268

Reuse Old Book 145

S

Section 268

    Assign Name 180–182, 268

    Change Start Page 268

    Continue Page Numbering 216, 225–226, 268

    Create 183–184, 269

    Delete 269

    Edit 269

    Insert Name 269

    Page Numbering 175, 183

Restart Page Numbering 182, 269

Section Breaks 97

Select All 36

Snapping 27, 62, 269

Spellcheck 139

Studio 269

    Definition 9–10

    Move or Anchor 269

    Preset Open 13

    Preset Save Changes 13

Studio Preset 270

    Add New 270

    Apply 270

    Delete 270

    Rename 270

    Save Changes 270

T

Table of Contents 270

    Entries

Formatting 163–165

Include Multiple Text Styles 161–162

Indent 166, 270

No Text Available 217, 271

Select 270

Update 270

For Section 271

Insert 158–160, 271

Multi-Page 174

Multiple 170–171, 173, 228–231

One-Level 155

Overarching 171, 173, 271

Page Numbers 162–163, 169, 271

Pre-Prep 156–158

Separators 166–169, 271

Update 169–170, 271

Templates 147

Text 272

Add 36–38, 46, 54, 75

Add Space Between Lines 272

Add Special Symbols or Characters 272

Alignment 272

All Caps or Small Caps 272

Apply Hyphenation 93, 113, 272

Apply Tracking 109–111, 113, 272

Bold 47, 273

Center Vertically 58

Edit 50

Font 36, 46, 273

Indent Paragraph 85, 273

Italics 273

Jump Image 47, 236, 273

Justification 93

Keep Together 273

Line Breaks 37

Line Spacing (Leading) 273

Move to Next Page 241–242, 274

Orphans Remove Automatically 95, 273

Orphans Remove Manually 109

Size 36, 274

Small Caps 274

Space Between Lines 56, 89

Special Characters 55

Underline 274

Weight 36, 274

Widows Remove Automatically 95, 274

Widows Remove Manually 109

Wrap Around Image 37, 39, 237, 274

Text Flow 274

Auto Flow 77–78, 274

Between Pages 72–73

From One Text Frame to Another

Add 274

Remove 275

From One Text Frame to
Another Add 69–72

Issues With 120

Unlink 137–138

Text Frame 275

Align or Position 27–28, 62,
275

Change Size 45

Copy and Paste 120

Insert 26, 54, 275

Overflow 76

Specify Width or Height 28

Text Style 275

Apply 91, 103, 275

Based On Other Style 275

Imported 275

Keyboard Shortcut 83, 275

Missing Italics 123

New 276

Update or Change 86, 276

Text Style Examples

Chapter Heading 89

First Paragraph 81–83

Main Body 85, 87

Thumbnail Size 22

Transform Studio 28, 33, 45

U

Undo 33

V

Videos

Affinity 2

ML Humphrey 147

W

Workspace

Customize 9–12

For Covers and Ads 13

For Print 12

ABOUT THE AUTHOR

M.L. Humphrey is a self-published author with both fiction and non-fiction titles published under a variety of pen names. When she gets stuck on her next fiction project she foolishly decides to write books that only ten people are going to buy, although she does usually learn something interesting in the process so it's worth it in the end.

You can reach her at:

mlhumphreywriter@gmail.com

or at

www.mlhumphrey.com

Printed in Great Britain
by Amazon

41706214R00165